Write Your Way To Happiness

Why you should start writing for your well-being today

By Alexandra Bădiță

©2018 by Alexandra Bădiță
Published by Impressivity by Alexandra
All rights reserved
Printed in Romania
ISBN 978-1-9999504-0-8

Cover by Laura Belc
Photo cover by Magdalena Gheorghe
Edited by Light Hurley
www.writeyourwaytohappiness.com

To my parents

Contents

Introduction

My relationship with writing began at an early age. I used to be a shy kid. So shy that I'd be hiding behind my mum's skirt when we would meet with strangers. At about 10 or 11, I started to put together rhymes and short stories about princesses and kingdoms. I attended numerous literature competitions in primary school. At some point, I slipped away from it. I only got to rekindle my love for writing in university. It was then that my parents were kind and supporting enough to allow me to choose the wild direction of journalism and advertising.

My first unpaid job was as a web editor for an online magazine. I moved on to a paid position by writing for the digital versions of magazines like Cosmopolitan or National Geographic. After being promoted to project manager, there was no more room for writing in my job description. Blogging became the answer for me. I would vent all my opinions and write about what was going on in my life. Especially in my dating life.

Back then, I had no idea how therapeutic it was for me to write about all those situations and share meaningful lessons with my readers. I was enjoying it nevertheless and the guys I would date were always feeling threatened and asking "Are you going to write about me?"

Not all of them made it on my blog, but at some point I decided to go even bigger and started writing for Elite Daily. Now that's a threat, if you screw with my heart.

Writing was indeed giving me a grip on things, but I wasn't yet aware about the inside patterns that were triggering all those stories. That is until one day, when I got so disconnected from myself and my feelings and everything and everyone around me that I hit rock bottom. After six months of walking around as if without sense or emotion, I ended up having a panic attack while I was home alone. As soon as I got back to my senses, I googled the closest therapist to my house and scheduled an appointment. I knew I needed help and it was time to get it.

I talk in this book about my entire experience in therapy - which was not long but quite intense - and how the writing exercises during the sessions helped me get back on track.

One other major lesson I learned - and is worth underlining here - is that we are all work in progress. Once we are back on track, it doesn't mean all is great. It means we need to stay aware, present, focused and always inwardly centred. We always need to work on ourselves and treat ourselves with the utmost love. And that's how my journey with personal development began...

There were times in my life when I thought I was a mess. There were times when I was blaming a higher power that I was not lucky enough to get what I wanted.

The truth was that the Universe had a bigger plan for me than I had for myself.

Moving to London brought me closer to this bigger plan. All the ups and downs have been part of the journey to my present self. Success and failure together have contributed in building me as the woman I am today.

I've always liked to share and show support, to somehow find the greater purpose of all this life. My journey towards coaching helped me find ways to channel my passions on a larger scale. And who knew it has been within me all along. In the form of pen and paper. And now to be shared as my first published book.

And I know this is only the beginning...

Alexandra Bădiță, London, December 2017

CHAPTER 1

What does Writing Therapy mean?

We live in a fast-pace society. Our lives rush on at a hundred miles per hour and we constantly feel pressure from mentalities that have put their stamp on us. Sooner or later, everyone goes through a mental breakdown, an episode of anxiety or fear. Many will hit rock bottom and deal with depression. Some might find their way back. Others will struggle for years and years with the dark side of their mind.

While the best way to overcome a tough time in your life is by facing it, we rarely find the determination or the knowledge straight away. If you are lucky and have some good friends, or you figure it out by yourself, you will be directed towards therapy, counselling, mentors or coaches.

Even though we live in a society where everyone struggles with mental health, it doesn't mean that we are more open to talk about it. That is where it all goes wrong, because if we were talking about it, so many lives would be changed. Instead, we tend to hide. We hide from ourselves, we hide for fear of being judged. If we do end up seeing a therapist, then God-forbid we ever confess this to anyone! Therapy is for crazy people, that's what we've been told while growing up. Therapy is when they tie you up with a long-sleeved shirt and lock you in a room with pillows on the walls.

These misconceptions keep traditional therapy taboo. We don't talk about it, even with our closest friends and family. Little do they know that therapy in fact gives you the tools to dig deep into your feelings and find the root of your problems. People tend to believe that going to therapy is like going to a guru: You'll spill the beans about your entire life and the therapist will magically solve everything. Well, it is important to keep in mind that the role of the therapist is not to sort out your life. No. Instead, the role of the therapist is to discover the source of your pain, what you need and give you the tools for you to do the work. No matter what kind of problem you're being supported through, whether moving on after loss or achieving goals you've been putting aside, you need to show up. You need to do the work with the tools provided. If you don't take part in the journey, you could just end up going for sessions for years and years and nothing will change. That is because your expectations are unrealistic. You are waiting for the solution to just show up in front of you. Remember. You cannot just sit on a couch and talk, you need to take action.

When I went to my first therapy session a few years back, I had no idea what to expect. I thought, just like pretty much everyone else, that I would lie down on a couch, speak about my pain and the therapist would say, "Why don't you do this and that?" And I would say back, "Oh my God, you are so right!" And then my mental health would be restored. And I would be back in the

12

game. Looking back, I couldn't have been more wrong. It wasn't a magical fix which was important in that first month, what was important was the tools and exercises that were given to me that helped me break through my patterns of thinking. If I hadn't taken action or realised that I am a continuous work in progress, none of the shifts would have happened.

This is where therapeutic writing comes into play. When you need to find a way to move forward, when you are motivated, you will take the necessary steps for healing. It's important that you are open to trying out what fits your needs and that you are paying attention to how each tool interacts with your mind.

You might have heard about alternative therapy methods. Most of the time these include different ways of expressing yourself in the way you feel most comfortable with. Art is very often used as an expression of self, an inner journey that the artist takes for self-discovery. Based on your skills and expertise, you might find yourself tempted to try out therapeutic methods like painting, sculpting, dancing or - why not - interior design or fashion. While they are all very useful ways to explore your inner self and to express yourself, there is one art that seems to be the most accessible and affordable: writing.

Don't get me wrong, I am a strong believer in investing in yourself, but some might be put off by the cost of a sculpting class or the prices of a high-quality canvas and brushes. The truth is, all you need for writing is a pen and a piece of paper. It couldn't be easier than this!

You may argue that while you have a pen and some paper, why not start drawing? Absolutely. If that's how you express yourself and you can do it, you should. It's brilliant. For me, however, and many of us, if you give us a pencil and paper we will think about writing instead of drawing. This is because we have all been taught to write and read from a young age and so for most people it will be a comfortable option. I personally have terrible drawing skills. I would never feel like I'm properly expressing my feelings with my attempts to put forms together on paper. With writing though, I can.

Writing is an art in itself. If you are truly inclined towards writing, you will want to explore the creative side of it, dive into fiction, build utopian worlds where your characters reflect your way of thinking. Some might struggle when coming up with an imaginative setup, a plot and characters. Instead, write from your heart. Write about what goes on in your mind. It is the *easiest* way to heal yourself and find your happiness.

When used for therapeutic purposes, writing is all about connecting your thoughts with your feelings. The way you feel in each and every moment of a day is determined by the thoughts that go through your head. Situations don't determine feelings, thoughts do. By understanding this and exploring this causality, you will be on the way to successful healing.

Thoughts and feelings go hand in hand in such a way that we don't see it on a daily basis. The second we become aware of this relation, we get to be in control of our thoughts. We can shift the way we feel and we can build our way to happiness. The same awareness and control will allow you to let go of what is not useful to you, what keeps you stuck and what makes you unhappy. The first step to all these major changes is being open and being willing to take action.

Writing can become part of your daily routine. The sooner you experience getting out of your head, the better. Taking one step back and seeing things objectively, while writing them down, will help you make sense of what is bothering you and where you need to work. Just stay present. Make sure you keep an open mind towards contradictory feelings that may arise throughout the journey. We are complex creatures. Our minds are wired in a complicated way. You might find that a thought generates both joy and worry or that there are multiple things that can contribute to your happiness in one single moment.

You need to stay true to the process and to yourself. The hand will translate whatever goes through your mind and put it into words. Identifying thoughts and writing them down will make sense of the feelings in your heart. It will even make sense of the physical sensations that go through your body.

You know that feeling in the pit of your stomach when you think about quitting your job? That is called fear, my dear. It is the body's reaction to your thought of generating change in your life. On a subconscious level, all the repercussions of this decision start unravelling. Your gut is built by default in safe mode, so it hurts when it is shaken. Without even realising, your thoughts are all about the bills you need to pay, the money and security this job offers you, the comfort of seeing the payroll at the end of the month. Yes, the comfort, because this is what it is about, that comfort zone that our gut wants to keep us in. It's cosy, it's safe, it's not risky. The body is accustomed to being comfortable and cosy. It doesn't want you to change anything. So it reacts. It makes you feel sick. It distracts you from the decision. This is where your work has to come into play.

Most people are not aware of the process above. They end up forgetting about their decision. However, you are not most people. Write it all down. Go through the process. Dig deeper and deeper. Then you'll realise that the feeling in the pit of your stomach is in fact fear, a fear that is waiting to be defeated. All you need to do is to take the risk, make the decision and quit that job. If it is what you truly want, you will find solutions to provide for yourself. This is something that we will explore in a future chapter of this book.

When I started teaching writing as a therapy method, people would be suspicious. I would explain to them that my purpose is not to judge the way they are feeling and what they are writing. My purpose is to show them a way of being their own therapists. Isn't that a good return of investment?

You don't have to be a writer in order to use writing therapy. By learning how to use writing to your own benefit, you will discover how this truly powerful tool can completely transform your life. When you become comfortable with facing your inner demons and writing them down, you will understand yourself better. You will be able to see your own worth and your own value. You will know how to put writing into practice as a way of lifting your spirits and creating a safe space for your thoughts and feelings. You will become your own therapist. You will become *the master of your own life.*

The truth is, writing is already part of your life. Whether you write an email, a shopping list or a Thank You card, you are putting a piece of yourself in that paragraph or on that paper. When you start practicing writing on a daily basis, it will become a habit. You will start feeling more connected, more grounded, more focused. All that mess you feel inside of you will start to make sense. It will reorganise. You will reconnect with your true feelings.

In order to get to the bottom of your feelings, you need to start asking yourself questions. Most of all, you need to be ready to give yourself honest answers. Without that honesty you cannot start the healing process. Of course, the most uncomfortable questions often trigger the deepest truths. You have to dig deeper than the surface, layer by layer, like peeling back an onion, to find your inner thoughts and patterns, and it is that which will cause the change. You will write those truths down. When you take a step back and look objectively at what you have uncovered, it will be earth-shattering. The true transformation waits at the deepest level. It waits beside the heart of the problem.

The most popular way of writing to yourself is journaling. Many people tend to keep a diary in their early years, when they feel like they are not understood by anyone, but drop out of the habit. Journaling is indeed one of the easiest ways to use writing, mainly because you can do it any way you want. You can write anything you want, you can be open, you can be ruthless. You also get to see change over time if you re-read it. Oh boy, realising how we grow up and how our thinking develops and changes can be overwhelming, but I promise you, it is amazingly helpful. I will dive deeper into journaling in one of the future chapters and we will explore the benefits of writing in a diary, as well as tips and tricks to make the most out of its potential.

While journaling is a way of writing just for yourself, I am also a strong believer in writing for sharing. Writing with the purpose of sharing is about shouting your story out to the world and making your point of view known. However, you don't need to project it on a large scale. You could just share it with that particular person you never got the chance to speak to. Maybe you want to ask for forgiveness, maybe they hurt you or maybe you were the one who caused the pain. Or perhaps you just want to let the other person know that you are thinking about them.

Sharing your thoughts in writing is powerful. People tend to get scared of it. The power of the written word is ten times greater than a spoken word. Written words tend to become heavier, potentially because we visualise the word and we imagine the intention of the tone. We can even keep these physical pieces of writing as legacy. It can be daunting.

Just by writing this book, I am aware that all I am putting down here is going to be out there in the world for everyone to read. There is no turning back. There is no chance to edit it once it hits the printer. But, at the thought of readers who will embark on a journey to explore their full potential because of this writing, all my worries fade away, and I continue typing with excitement.

Writing with the purpose of sharing gets you to start facing fears that you have been avoiding since this morning, since a few days or even years ago. You might get to share the writing with the person your writing is about or you can choose to let a wider audience have a peek into your story. Stories bring people together. There is always someone else going through something similar. Not everyone is willing to share their take on the situation, but everyone finds comfort in realising they are not alone.

When you start writing, the highest revelation is the sense of freedom. The truth is we hold onto emotions for too long. We become trapped, just like how those emotions are trapped in us. Maybe we want to get rid of them, but we don't know how. So we just keep revisiting them over and over again. We keep bringing them to life, never releasing them. How would you feel if I told you that writing down your emotions will get you that freedom you have been craving? When putting your pen to paper it will feel like unlocking a cage of doves, setting them free, never to be seen again. Can you imagine how much lighter you would feel? How much space you would be freeing up, just like clearing a memory stick, making room for new files and documents, in the form of emotions and experiences?

Life can sometimes be an unfair deal. There are so many occasions when we are left with words unsaid. Just think of this scenario: you get into an argument with your partner. They say all these mean things to you, they blame you for things you didn't even know about and they throw at you all this guilt. You just give up trying to reciprocate. Or maybe you just don't like arguing and prefer to shut up and close yourself up. Or they just walk out on you and slam the door behind them, without even giving you the opportunity to explain. Wouldn't it be nice to actually get to speak your mind and get a chance to tell your side of the story?

In any argument, conflict or situation, there are always two sides of the coin. We may not always get to tell our side if the other person is more assertive or just has a louder voice. All those unspoken words will eventually get to the surface when you least expect it. You may end up bursting in a completely random circumstance due to this accumulation of anger and frustration. You can already guess what I am about to say. You need to write it out! Write your thoughts! Write all the words you wanted to say to the other person and make your voice heard! Share it with the person who did you wrong. Share it with the person who maybe you did wrong to. If you didn't get the chance to speak up during the situation itself, take your turn now. Express your side of the coin, how it looks from your perspective.

So what is there to do? Start writing! Start writing straight away. Just sit down and write whatever comes to your mind. Write continuously for one minute, then for two minutes and so on. Just start small. You will build your "writing muscle". Write without interruption. Write with curiosity. Write to see what will come out of it at the end of the exercise. Write to explore your thoughts at that particular time. Just make a pact with yourself to keep the pencil running on the paper without a break. Don't worry about editing or making your writing easy to read. Just practice the act of writing. Write, write, write!

In case you do want to review what you wrote, I advise you not to do it straight away. After you finish writing, put the piece of paper or the notebook aside. Don't think about it. Get back to it either at the end of the day or the next day. You will see it with a fresh perspective, with a little bit of objectivity if you may. You will understand it better and it will make sense.

If you wonder what the immediate benefit in starting to write straight away is, just think about this: you deserve two minutes a day to just connect with yourself. You won't even realise how much good will come out of those two minutes.

Writing will get you to sit in one place and focus on one thing. And that thing will be *you*. You will be focused on what is going on inside of you and writing it down. You will be present. You will be grounded, focused, mindful. Once you finish the exercise you will feel like a rock has been lifted off your chest. You will feel that sense of freedom creeping up your veins and, once you have a taste of the freedom that writing provides, you will be addicted. You will want to release all those feelings from your soul and your mind. You will crave those two minutes of writing every day. Then, those two minutes will become three. Then five. Then ten, and then you just won't feel the need to look at your watch, because you will be the pen running on that paper.

So what are you waiting for? Grab your pen and make sure it has enough ink. Sharpen your pencil. Find a blank sheet of paper. There's a special space dedicated for this at the end of the book. Or use a napkin, I don't really care. Just start writing for heaven's sake!

CHAPTER 2

Benefits of Writing as Therapy

Without realising its true power, writing has been used throughout the years for therapy. It was only fairly recently that research bloomed in this direction and the potential of writing became an interest for cognitive behavioural scientists.

Please note that writing as therapy doesn't replace prescribed medication or treatment for diagnosed patients with depression. It can however be used as a complementary activity for ongoing recovery and well-being and it is advised for you to seek specialised medical care and consultation if you feel constantly depressed, anxious or if you experience self-harming thoughts.

Now let's have a look at all the benefits writing can have in your life.

1. Physical Health

Considered to have been one of the pioneers of the way writing is tied to both physical and mental health, Professor James W. Pennebaker has conducted numerous studies and extensive research on this topic.

One of his early studies, which is now known as the Pennebaker method, involved a number of students who were asked to write about a traumatic experience of their lives for 20 minutes every day, for four consecutive days. Another group was asked to write about a neutral topic with no involvement of expressing their feelings. The results showed that the first group visited their doctor less in the following six months, that the release of stress on paper had positively impacted their immune system.

This study proves one of the theories that Pennebaker was suspecting to be true ever since he had started studying the power of words. Writing improves not only mental health, but also physical health.

Another study was performed with two groups of different age ranges, both including men and women. The objective was to understand how writing impacts people's lives based on their age. When they were instructed to write about the difficulties in their present lives and what gives them anxiety, the exercise started revealing various concerns. Elder people were worried about their health, their retirement, their children and grandchildren. The younger generation were worried about exams, not knowing where to apply for college or why they were single.

Regardless of the nature of their worries, both groups reported an improvement in their mood after the writing exercise.

Expressing feelings on paper is more than just putting words into a sentence. It's also the way you put it, the words you choose, the aspects of the situation that you choose to focus on.

Pennebaker was also noting the language used by the people who participated. For the first four days in a row, the participants of the test reflected at first from their own point of view, using "I". Later, they moved on to using the third person, therefore proving that they began to see events from different perspectives and angles. In fact, one of the conditions that make writing successful or not is to start thinking about and expressing events differently. There will be no change in our health if we keep saying the same things, telling ourselves the same negative advice or using the same language. In order to see improvement, there must be change.

You may notice that when you first begin writing to share, you will only scribble about shallow things. You might find yourself being afraid to go in depth and explore the feelings hidden behind the surface of the issue. It does indeed require strength of will to face the fears and unspoken words, but it is definitely worth it. In time you will discover that your analytical senses will come into play more often. You will start exploring your thoughts and feelings from different angles and you will see the transformation. It is then when writing will start to produce its miracles. It is then that writing will become your go-to activity for stress relief.

Most researchers explain the process by the simple fact that seeing the bothering story in front of you, presented by sentences, makes it an outside world. There is a switch. It is no longer just inside. You take a step back. You look at it from a new perspective. It is no longer subjective and you are no longer alone, isolated with your thoughts. Rather the account becomes a narrative in a book, like a story, and you are just a witness, you are seemingly not involved. You read it. You look at it. You watch it unravel. You let it go.

The fact of the matter is, regardless of age or gender, people encounter a wide range of stress factors. This is of course not to be judged. We are not meant to be judging ourselves or others, we are not here to become someone else's therapists, only our own therapist. By choosing to practice this writing exercise, you can see whether it gives you an immediate boost in your happiness levels, be it only by a slight acknowledgement of the circumstances or by realising that the degree to which it concerns us is not as high as we initially thought when we were keeping it to ourselves. We write it down and alternative scenarios start developing in our heads. It's understandable that stress is being relieved.

It is also common that you might experience emotional discomfort once you start writing about a painful event or a trauma. You are, after all, re-living the emotions and the impact of events. That can be overwhelming. In most cases, this discomfort starts to go away in the following couple of hours after the writing exercise.

However, you must be aware that writing doesn't work for everyone. If you feel that it is not your cup of tea, you can try out other methods of healing or seek help from a specialist. As professor James W. Pennebaker put it himself in the interview he offered me, "The one potential problem is that some people occasionally get into a ruminative cycle where they process the same negative issues over and over and over again. Indeed, rumination is a sign of depression. This is one reason that I recommend that people start off writing a limited number of times – perhaps three or four."

Exercise: write for five minutes about a situation that causes you stress. Explore all its aspects, how it makes you feel and what you have to do in order to diminish the impact of that stress. You have space dedicated at the end of the book that you can use for this exercise.

---

2. Mindfulness

Writing is closely related to mindful activity. I've always seen writing as the action that grounds me in the present. This is because when I write I need to keep my thoughts together in one line in order to be able to catch them in phrases that make sense. Therefore they start making sense in my head too. You can't just run your fingers over your computer's keyboard just for the sake of it without the intention to form words or letters or numbers that have a meaning. You need coherence. When you write you are therefore thinking about what comes out of your hands.

It's even more challenging - and more pleasant I might add - when it comes to using good old-fashioned pen and paper. Given that handwriting tends to be slower than typing, you need to be even more focused in order to not lose track of your thoughts. You need to stay with your story, thoughts, feelings and sensations in order to make sure you are not missing a single thing when you write it down.

It is also true that the sound of a pen or pencil running on a piece of paper can be very soothing. It keeps you connected to the act of writing, just like the sound of typing can keep you from getting distracted. I personally prefer listening to music when writing - smooth jazz or some soothing piano in the background - but it is the tactile sense that keeps me in touch with the activity of writing. I get to feel my fingers hitting each key on the laptop's keyboard. I get to feel how my hand holds the pencil and the way that the piece of paper feels when I turn the page. My connection with writing keeps me in the present moment through sensorial experience.

What I am trying to prove here is that the whole body engages in the act of writing. If we pay attention, not only do all the senses play an important role in the process, but so too do our muscles. We are kept engaged, awake and present. Mindfulness is about keeping the mind present, but the experience can be fully enriching when the body comes to complete the action in itself. The hand muscles are active - the fingers, the forearm etc. - making a call to the shoulder blades to keep them in position so our upper body can stay focused. My opinion is that the body has to be awake and comfortable at the same time. It's up to you if you feel better with your feet touching the ground, cross-legged or standing. Choose whichever position feels good to you in that particular moment.

3. Structure

Another major benefit of writing is one I've briefly mentioned before, and that is ordering one's thoughts.

Our minds are extremely busy. Our thoughts, concerns, predictions keep us always alert, sometimes to a point where they don't even allow us to sleep properly. I like to think of the human mind as a highway at rush hour, where the cars are our thoughts and they drive around buzzing, making a mess and most of the time disturbing the peace of what should be a quiet one-way street.

In meditation practice, the human mind that is restless and that fights against silence is known as a monkey mind, the mind that just jumps from tree to tree. This is normal. We are prone to thinking and overthinking. Our minds are wired in a way that the circuits are always alive. There is always at least one thought going through the pipes. We have to admit it's a challenge to keep our minds quiet and focused. You know what they say though - practice makes perfect. Regular practice of meditation, stress-relief methods and mindfulness will make our mind more obedient when we turn down the volume.

When we sit down and proceed to write, we make it a bit easier to focus. If we isolate all other things going on around us - for instance if you are in a busy coffee place, just ignore the sound of the coffee machine or the music in the background. Instead focus on what you want to write. This is like a slow-speed car on the highway. We take it for a drive, then we leave it, pick another one and drive it until we discover another one. It is how the story starts to unfold on the paper.

Sometimes we find ourselves in complicated situations. Sometimes we just can't see the light at the end of the tunnel. Our thoughts become so entangled that there seems to be no way out of the mess. This is the best time to practice writing. This is when it will make the most sense to organise whatever goes through your head. Professor Pennebaker explains: ""By writing, you put some structure and organisation to those anxious feelings. It helps you to get past them". This is the best moment to sit down and face all those potential problems that may not even be true, problems which, because they live in your head, seem impossible to solve. Try this when you feel overwhelmed, although it might be the last thing on earth you want to do. Sit down and write everything down that bothers you when you feel the burden. Do it. See how it makes you feel. See what solutions you might end up finding and how you see things afterwards. You might end up being surprised.

While the above benefits can be easily spotted even when you are a beginner in writing, there are many more that will be unravelled once you start frequently writing.

4. Self-observation

If you keep a record of some recurring situations and the way you react in those circumstances, you will start observing patterns of behaviour. One of the best ways to see these patterns is through journaling. Keeping a journal can show how similar situations trigger similar thoughts and feelings. By keeping track and analysing, you become aware of these patterns and you can take the next step to change them.

Without even knowing, we react in the same way when we encounter similar circumstances. Due to our so-called "rules of living" we tend to protect ourselves, instead of being open to new situations, by repeating the ways we react. These patterns are so well ingrained into our being they are known as habits. We don't even realise what triggers the burst, we just react. It might not be a similar situation, but even a similar factor might evolve into something new. We don't have the patience to wait. We just react.

Take for instance failed relationships. Let's say a woman has experienced a number of relationships that ended up with her partners cheating on her. She therefore sees all potential future partners as cheaters. She immediately builds up a wall around her to protect her feelings and maybe keeps herself away from commitment. Even if she does meet a good guy who is loyal and shows no sign of being interested in other women, she will still react the same to the slightest sign of misunderstanding. She has a pattern of reacting with jealousy. She assumes that all situations are the same, that all guys will cheat on her. Instead of taking each situation as it is, and giving a fresh chance to a new guy, she just expects all relationships to have the same ending. She has already formed a pattern of reaction and a defence mechanism.

When it comes to writing and journaling, you might revisit what you have written previously in similar situations. Then, instead of reacting out of habit, you become aware of the trigger by taking a step back to look at the circumstances with a fresh approach.

It will come easier with time. And it will also allow us to understand the relation between thoughts and feelings better. In our daily routine, we are not aware of the way feelings are triggered by our own thoughts. We might feel a multitude of emotions in relation to one single event, but how could we know? We end up being confused and overwhelmed. If we write it down, we start making sense of the emotions that each thought brings. We begin identifying how a single fact can make us feel both happy and sad, based on the thoughts that go through our heads at that moment. By understanding this process, we can be in control of our thoughts. We can change them to positive alternatives that give us positive emotions. I'm sure you've heard the phrase "think happy thoughts". Maybe you've mocked it before, but guess what? It works. If we program our mind to think positive, we end up being positive and living happily. Isn't this what we are all looking for?

As proof of the relation between thoughts and feelings, try the exercise below. It is the exercise that has in fact been the closest to my heart in my own journey and it explores exactly this correlation.

The STaF Exercise: Divide a piece of paper into three columns. The first column will be the Situation, the second column will be the Thoughts and the third column will be the Feelings. Put down in the first column a situation that has already happened or a future event that you are planning to go through with. Then write in the second column the thoughts that cross your mind that are related to that particular event. There maybe a trickle of thought, there might be a waterfall. The thoughts may be harmonious or the thoughts may conflict. Let them come. Don't censor yourself. Put it all down. Lastly, connect a feeling by writing it down in the third column. Be it positive or negative, there might be a number of feelings that start unravelling once your thoughts are set free.

Situation	Thoughts	Feelings

So far, we have been exploring a number of benefits. I'm sure that if you take the time to complete the exercises suggested so far, you will start seeing small changes in your thinking and in your mood. It's your first step towards happiness, so why delay it?

5. Anger release

If you're still having trouble thinking about happiness and well-being, it might be that you are going through a tough time in your life at the moment. Most of the time, negative events tend to leave us angry and our rage manifests in a multitude of ways. We may be angry about the people that cause us harm, we may be angry about people who are really innocent. We may be angry against divinity or we may even be angry about ourselves. Dealing with anger - especially when it is a long-time anger - can be challenging, but not impossible.

Just like in our previous section on the benefits of writing, it is about letting the anger go. If you express your anger in writing instead of keeping it inside, you will be relieved. You won't take it to the dear ones who just happen to be around you at the wrong time. You yourself get to be freed from the clenching power of rage. All the negative energy that otherwise remains stored in your mind and in your body gets released on paper.

Most of the time, we get angry when people do something wrong that affects us in a direct or indirect way. We may not get a chance to tell the other person how they did us wrong or what our opinion is about their actions. Instead of releasing the negative feelings or solving the conflict through conversation, we accumulate the negative thoughts and feelings that sooner or later will explode. The danger of this is that it might end up affecting other innocent people in our lives. Most of all we end up hurting ourselves by making ourselves feel guilty as well, thinking less of ourselves. Anger is the worst enemy of our self-worth. When we lack someone to blame, we end up blaming ourselves. We keep telling ourselves the story over and over again until we believe it. The damage done can still be reversible, but why not prevent it in the first place? It is said that depression is anger turned inwards, so why allow it to develop in the first place?

When something happens in your life that makes you feel angry, write it down. Put it on paper. Imagine all the things you would tell the other person to relieve that negativity from your core. Don't let it rot inside.

Even if you don't get to share it with the person that did you wrong, the simple act of releasing the anger on paper will make you feel like a new person. Your heart and mind will be lighter. If you are lucky enough to get the chance to share the piece of writing with the person at the opposite end of the story, it might turn out to be a good lesson for them.

6. Sharing lessons

This brings us to another benefit of writing. Sharing our stories is a good way of sharing lessons and knowledge. There are times in our lives that we might learn stuff the hard way, but we eventually got there. When we drag the line and look back, we realise that instead of going about it through the long way, we might have taken the shortcut, if only someone had told us. So maybe it's us who needs to share the shortcut with someone else, someone who needs it and who is in the same dark place we once were.

There is a study conducted in 2010 at Bristol University revealing that we learn from our mistakes by repeating them over and over again, but we learn faster from other people's mistakes. So if we get a chance to write down an event, a bad experience or a situation that led to a negative ending, then we should do it. It's our duty to share our stories with other people who might benefit from our struggle and the solution we eventually found. Why let them struggle? They might find your piece of advice useful. They might benefit from it in a way that you might not even intend. Writing and sharing, needless to say, brings people together. It unites them in a way that is not easy to see at first, and it confirms that we are not alone in this world.

7. Means of communication

There is no doubt that writing is a tool of communication. And by that I mean communicating short or long distance, for good or bad news, for flirting, arguing, complimenting, apologising or inviting. Before telephones or even telegraphs were invented, long distance communication was always done by sending letters, even though there was a discrepancy between the moment when the letter was written and sent to the moment it was delivered. Writing has undoubtedly been the most reliable way of distributing news across short or long distances. Besides, in the absence of anything else, why would anyone question the efficiency of writing?

Confidentiality has kept its validity nowadays too, as it is the privacy of messaging, texting or emailing that gives private writing a better reputation than publicly communicating matters that shall only remain private. On top of the efficiency and confidentiality of words that might otherwise remain unspoken, writing also gives various hints about the writer's personality and mood by the tone of voice, the emphasis on certain words or the punctuation - or in modern days, the emojis they use.

All these contribute to delivering a message that expresses in a concise way some words - good or bad - that the writer might be more comfortable to offer by writing.

It sometimes is the case that written words can be considered heavier by the receiver, as they see the word and it may carry a different meaning for them than for the writer. Plus, in the absence of body language, texts or emails can be easily misinterpreted. Letters on the other hand have the benefit of being more elaborate. They give the opportunity to the writer to express themselves better, more explicitly, and on as many pages as they want. Living in such a dynamic world though means also choosing shorter and faster forms of communication in writing, which can then be followed up with phone calls or face-to-face meetings.

8. Visualisation

Another benefit of writing is the relationship it has with the capability of visualising. As mentioned earlier in this chapter, there are a million things going through our heads.

A good way to make sense out of it is by writing it down and deciphering it. When writing it down, you see that place, you visualise it to its smallest details, if you wish, and you make it extremely visible through your mind's eye. The big advantage of visualisation in writing is that you can create a context, you can describe and flesh out its most important parts. Writing can get you to travel back in time, remembering a sweet or bitter memory, or writing can send you to the future, a goal, an objective that you have dreamt of.

When it comes to the memories that we chose to write down on paper, the opinions of specialists and researchers are divided. Some people consider that happy moments are only to be remembered by memory. Sonja Lyubomirsky underlines this statement in her book *How of Happiness* by saying that writing about the past has the purpose of healing. For Lyubomirsky, writing is best referred to for recalling traumatic experiences and negative thoughts, whereas happy memories can lose their positive touch once we focus too much on the details and start writing them down.

On the other side of the coin, *The Little Book Of Hygge* by Meik Wiking makes an important point when it says that putting happy experiences on paper makes your soul relive the moments and treasure them further. Either way, just write.

9. Forgiveness

We've already touched on the point of writing for the purpose of releasing anger, but another way is to also use this magic tool to make peace and forgive. There are times when you need to make peace either with yourself or with other people and it can be equally important and difficult. You will realise that the exercise will make you feel lighter. Even if the other person doesn't ask for forgiveness, you are in a place of healing and don't want to hold grudge. Instead you choose to come to peace with the situation. I know what you are thinking. I agree with you. It is damn difficult and challenging and it will take time, but writing through the pain will make the situation easier.

In addition, you will feel more in control of your thoughts and you will realise that you are the master of your own mind. Thoughts don't hold authority over you. You are the one who can choose whether to hold a grudge or to get over it. You are the one who has the power to heal your soul and live in well-being and happiness.

Summing up the points listed as benefits of writing in this chapter, I want to remind you once again to write.

38

When we keep it all in our own heads, we see everything through the filter of our past experiences. Instead of keeping it all in a subjective light and being stubborn about it, the simple act of writing helps us take a step back and see it all from a different point of view. We detach ourselves from the situation and we become witnesses of our own story. Sometimes we can even explore a variety of sides to the story. You won't even know how it looks like from the outside until you write it down. So what are you waiting for?

CHAPTER 3

Writing to heal from trauma

Writing is included in most therapy sessions. Yes, you don't usually see it in the movies when the characters of the story end up going to counselling, but that is where the misconception of therapy comes from. We have to do 90 percent of the work on ourselves when going through a difficult time. Therapists are there to guide us. They are there to offer us tools and a safe place where we can open our hearts. But, at the end of the day, it is still on us. Writing gives us a chance to be honest with ourselves in a way that we may not be able to with others.

Therapists sometimes practice by encouraging their patients to take notes during the sessions to make them more receptive and more present through their journey of healing. In most cases, people find it difficult to confess to their therapists their deeper feelings due to the fear of being judged. Therefore, these beliefs must be somehow taken into consideration and brought to the attention of the patient when they surface. It's then when writing might become useful.

Speaking about traumatic experiences in therapy sessions is one of the most challenging parts of healing.

Acknowledging what went wrong, how someone hurt us or how we hurt someone requires a lot of work. This is the main reason why therapists recommend particular exercises where the patient writes as they dig deep into their subconscious.

Sometimes we may be in such deep denial that we don't even recall some negative experiences in our lives, due to how well we buried them instead of dealing with the pain:

> "Carrying anything over from the past becomes a burden. In order to live fully in the present, we have to lay down that burden. And in order to do that, we have to know what things we carry with us."
> - *The Dynamic Way of Meditation* by **Dhiravamsa**.

It is important to be aware that the process of writing through trauma is hard. The journey may start in pure darkness, scary and ugly, but, once we decide to take the road towards healing and trust the process, the light at the end of the tunnel will show up. Of course, a big part of work has to be done on the inside. It must come with an open mind and with curiosity. There will be several stages. Each of them will bring us closer to healing. It will not be easy. Unless it is driven by a strong determination and willingness to overcome, an exploration of pain will take a long time.

Some people - myself included - find it useful to combine writing for healing with meditation in order to keep focused on the purpose, to make sure that we are determined to overcome the burden that's hanging over our heads.

The main fear that freezes people's willingness to heal themselves is the pain of reliving the past. They find it so painful to go back in time and remember a situation and the feelings associated with it that they sometimes choose to just ignore it and leave it there. Yes, it is painful. As I mentioned in a previous chapter, reliving a trauma will probably trigger all the painful emotions associated with the trauma as well. But, it does work. And it takes work, sweat and tears. When you choose to write about a difficult experience that has marked your life, you go back into the moment, feel those feelings all over again and revisit the scene. All of a sudden you can be back in your childhood when you were abused or back in that college dorm room when you were insulted or aggressed. One thing is for sure, this process will take time and you have to be patient and take your time with it. Don't force things. Maybe you won't be able to break the patterns and barriers with the first attempt, but you have to keep trying. It will pay off.

The first stage of attempt can take as long as is needed. When you eventually break through the pain, your release will be right around the corner. Once you manage to rewind the tape and go through what has happened, you will start feeling free. You will start understanding the context and you will release yourself from guilt. You might even forgive the other person or persons involved.

Writing it all down will help you see that you are now in a safe place. You have grown so much from the time it went wrong. You will break through the pain and you will feel the heaviness lifting from your chest. It will become clear and the light at the end of the tunnel will just become bigger and bigger.

The pain has not left because the feelings are still there, somewhere deep down. No matter how hard we try to ignore them and pretend that they don't affect us, some thoughts might resurface when we least expect it. They may transform and release in random situations, just like a pot of tea brought to boil which steams. Anger, tension or negative energy accumulated over time will look to get outside at some point. It will be difficult to become aware of the real cause behind the outburst, but it can affect us and our relationships with the people around us. And it will come back over and over again if we don't reach its roots and heal it.

Body sensations associated with the experience might also be felt again. During the healing process, you might start to notice how the once painful memory will cause less and less of a clench in your stomach or less and less heaviness in your heart.

"Finding meaning in the trauma through writing also seems to reduce how often and how intensely we experience intrusive thoughts about it," mentions Sonja Lyubomirsky in her book *The How Of Happiness*. "It makes sense that if writing helps people find a modicum of meaning and resolution in their trauma, they might find their emotional reactions to it more manageable and might be less disturbed by unwanted ruminations."

The process of letting it all go on paper contributes big time to your healing. Getting it all off your chest is the first step towards your soul transformation. You will find yourself fidgeting and maybe telling the story of what happened from a top level, just as an overview of the facts from the fear of going into the painful details. Try the exercise over and over again until you start feeling comfortable with pen and paper. Make them your best friends, your confidents. Trust them. Once you start being more at ease with putting your hard times into words and offering them as a gift to the paper in front of you, you will begin feeling like a spectator of the happening. You will be the "fly on the wall" while the facts unfold in front of you. And, though you will refrain from judging what is going on, emotions will inevitably arise and maybe even physical sensations, like nausea or the feeling of your heart breaking into a million pieces or a knife stabbing through your heart. These are all normal. As painful as they will be, you will become used to them and will eventually see the benefit of reliving them.

It is a way of beginning to accept them as past experiences, things that cannot harm us anymore. It is all in the past. Although it may not have been in our control when it happened, now it is in our control to come to peace with it. Just as professor Lyubomirsky explains, "The very act of writing sentences may prompt you to think in causal terms, thereby triggering an analysis that could help you find meaning, enhanced understanding and ultimately a sense of control."

If you see yourself in a position of being too far away from the roots of the events after writing, ask yourself some additional questions that will help you peel off the layers. Why did this person react like this? How did I feel? How did it make the other people around react? When was the first time I thought about it? What was going on through my mind at that very moment? What was going through my head after the event? How did my body react? What was my first response to the situation?

These questions should help you find powerful answers to the feelings deep down in your soul. Once you get there, it will make sense out of the mess in your head and heart. You will start seeing clearly what needs to be changed. Just remember to treat it all with kindness. Be gentle to yourself. Allow yourself all the time it takes to break through the pain.

First and foremost, allow yourself time for grief. This is something that many people ignore or skip because they just want to jump into healing and get it over with as soon as possible. If only it worked like this...

The conclusion I'm trying to get to is that you can't rush the healing process. It will take as long as it will take. Otherwise, there will remain feelings that haven't been dealt with and they will eventually re-surface. It is important to be careful with grief and be patient. Every person is unique. Each of us deals with grief in our own time and in our own way. We choose the tools and ways that fit our personality, our world, our beliefs. We deal with reality at our own pace. The most important thing to remember from this is that grief is part of the coping and accepting stage that will eventually result in healing.

So, as much as you wish to skip the pain and rush into the healing process, don't. All you will achieve is frustration that it didn't work. Even when you write it down it is difficult to get to the bottom of it when it is too early.

Pain manifests in a multitude of ways. You may think you are ready, that your pain didn't affect you deeply, but you might miss some deeper emotions. From personal experience, I would advise to stay with the pain at first. Make it flow through you before you choose to push it away. Of course, we all wish to take the shortcut and cure ourselves as fast as possible. Some cases are easier to get over than others. Difficulties hit us harder if we are in a less stable emotional state. Write through the process if you find it brings you calm and release. At the same time don't fight resistance to the writing process. Stay with it. Take your time. I just can't emphasise this enough.

Traumatic experiences, losses, failures or negative events that we can't control might make us feel unworthy. Any of these circumstances can threaten our self-worth. They give us negative feelings and then we feed this negativity. We will address this attack to our self-esteem later in this book in a separate chapter. What is important to keep in mind at this stage is that writing down the internal chatter will help us see patterns.

When you are alone, before going to bed or when you are commuting or sitting on the toilet, what do you tell yourself? Be aware of the inner accusations if they arise. You are probably so used to it that you might not even notice it at first. You will just be convinced that whatever you are telling yourself is true. Guess what? Your mind can trick you. Once you face it and go through healing, it is your turn to trick it.

Writing down the stuff you tell yourself will help you notice the cycle of thoughts and the instinctive reply your mind has to a situation that is repeating. It is most common for people to blame themselves, to keep saying "It's my fault, I always screw up". Just notice this and write it down. When you read back your entries in the notebook, pay attention to the repetitions. Which thoughts come up more often? Is it a kind and gentle tone? Or is it continuous shooting of accusations? Just notice the cycle. Make sure you make the conscious decision to change it.

You now desire to see things differently. You want to turn toward a more encouraging and empowering internal talk. Once you start modifying your patterns, things will start to brighten up. Motivation will be the main driver of your thoughts. Soon you will begin to be motivated by the desire to break those patterns and leave the cycle of low self-esteem behind. Take notes through the process of change. Notice how it makes you feel. Give it a fresh meaning. Write down your new ways of seeing things and you will be surprised by how accurate they are. You will understand you are on the right way.

You see, when you keep telling yourself that you are guilty, even if it isn't true, you will start believing it. It can even be the case that you will have the tendency to blame divinity in the absence of finding a specific reason or person to blame. This will disrupt the energy that should be otherwise supporting you from the higher power. Besides, you will fail to see the signs that the Universe sends you.

When you focus all your attention on guilt and all things negative, you will not be able to spot any support that comes your way. You will be so entrenched that it will take a few more steps before the Universe will make an obvious attempt to give you a helping hand. Truth is, you really need to break through the cycle before you can even start believing in a higher power. Soon you will see how it supports you unconditionally. It is that well-known law of attraction that screws us up. Once the action has been taken for a positive perspective, it will start being more obvious for you. The secret throughout this journey is to keep believing. Don't blame the Universe. Trust it. It will offer you what you need and what you ask for.

By this point we've drawn the roadmap of the post-traumatic stages. Grief needs to be the first step. Remember to take your time with this stage. Once the grief starts lowering its intensity you will move into a different level of awareness. You will notice patterns, you will take note of the things you tell yourself and you will reach a breakthrough. From then on, you can start transforming your emotions associated with the traumatic event and you can start seeing things from a new point of view. You can begin the healing.

What follows is the magic path towards release and the first rays of happiness. It will proceed with the process of purification. The simple action of letting go of emotions on paper will give you relief. Once you get accustomed with pen and paper in the pursuit of purification, you can lean on other tools.

If you recognize the writing as being painful but necessary, you can try this: write whatever is on your mind that you need to let go of and burn that piece of paper. Imagine the paper has become the problem you wrote on it and that when it burned away the problem also burned away. It will give you that purification. This will be an instant release; a method of purification.

Try practicing self-compassion. Be kind to yourself, stay connected within. Once you feel ready, you can release yourself through forgiveness. This step seems challenging but once you understand how it works, it will make more sense. Forgiveness is not about forgiving the other person, it is about releasing yourself from the event and freeing space in your heart and mind. One of my mentors, Professor Raj Raghunathan, discusses this in his online course about "A life of happiness and fulfilment" and in his book *If You're So Smart, Why Aren't You Happy?* He said during our interview, "The most important thing about forgiveness is that you are doing it more for yourself and not for the other person. I think many people have the idea of them having been wronged and the other person has to do something to restore the sense of fairness between them. But this is counterproductive because the other person will not do something just because you are angry and you will instead be angry for a longer time. Just let go and move on. Being angry with someone is like allowing someone to live in your mind rent-free."

Professor Raghunathan suggests you can try writing a letter on why the other person behaved in the way they did. This way you try to empathise with their situation:

"Had I been in their shoes, I might have behaved the same. Even though you hurt me, I forgive you."

One of the most practical long-term purifications is journaling. Writing down thoughts post trauma requires consistency when seen as an ongoing process. It also keeps track of the purification process throughout time and the evolution can be amazing. Again, this is the type of process you don't want to rush. You want to become used to writing and make it part of your life. You want to see it as a choice, not as a burden. You want to make use of it in your interest and not make yourself become a slave of a journal that forces you to write down an entry just because it is a task you have to do.

Journaling is the tool of choice for people who want to stay grounded and release their feelings of trauma in writing. In fact, it is no secret that many of the famous leaders of the world had one thing in common and that is the fact that they were keeping a journal. It is no wonder that journaling has offered so many benefits to people suffering not only from traumatic experiences but from mental illnesses, and that the writing influenced their perception of reality.

Virginia Woolf for example was diagnosed with bipolar disease. Her journals later became sources of inspiration in her fiction writing. After all, fiction is also therapy in itself for the writer, as they can hide their own feelings and personality in fictional characters under the excuse that they live in a fantasy world. Such a great disguise for a painful reality. Also on her side are authors like Mark Twain, F. Scott Fitzgerald and Sylvia Plath.

They are but a few on the list of famous names that fought with mental illnesses through writing.

As far as I am concerned, the most powerful and emotional journal I have read so far remains *The Diary of Anne Frank*. It has been an emotionally challenging decision to finish reading this book and it took longer than it should have, but it felt so emotionally draining with every turn of the page. Maybe it was because it was a journal and not a piece of fictional writing, making it feel more real and keeping me aware that its stories did really happen, that the writer did really go through those feelings described without even knowing what was about to happen. On top of all that, perhaps it was the fact that I felt like intruding into someone else's intimacy and privacy by reading their journal, knowing that it was all true. What stayed with me at the end of the book, in between tears, was one of Anne Frank's quotes: "Paper has patience". It is so unbelievably true and proves the fabulous power of writing.

Nevertheless, we all know that journals are not meant for the public eye. That is why we choose to be open and honest with our confident. If you are fearless and want to really let your story out for good, you can choose to write and share.

One of the most powerful exercises that help people deal with feelings caused by an event that involved another person is writing a letter. Write to a person who hurt you, whether they are dead or alive. Write down everything that has been bothering you. Write it regardless of what you do with it afterwards. You can send it or not. You can throw it away, you can burn it or you can publish it. The true healing is in the process of writing and then it is up to you what you do with it.

Just remember, take your time and never react from impulse. In fact, the right way to do it is to respond and not react. Reaction comes from patterns of behaviour, but in the purification process we have already broken through those patterns and cycles and we are seeing things clearly, we are responsive to what happens to us. Write your responses, write your inner chatter, write and observe, be honest and be aware. What do you notice?

CHAPTER 4

Writing for the awareness of feelings

In the scientific community, there are continuous arguments about whether the mind sits in the brain or if the mind is part of the human soul influencing the entire body. On the most basic level, we often hear about the left side of the brain being responsible for rational thinking, whereas the right part of the brain is emotional. There are neurons running and jumping around, there are synapses connecting them and there is all this storage space for memories and learnings.

However, the space is limited. I remember watching some cartoons when I was little and seeing in one of the episodes an explanation of how the space in a mind is divided similarly to a chest of drawers. When they get full, the mind starts throwing away the unnecessary memories or things that we wish to remember.

All thoughts trigger feelings and body sensations. It's universally acknowledged that the mind has so many thoughts going on around that it creates a constant buzz in between our ears.

I like to imagine that the thoughts in our head are like the cars on the highway at rush hour. They don't follow any traffic rules, they just create a traffic jam if we don't pay attention.

Even at times when our mind seems to be packed, our brains are trained to only think one thought at a time. Just pay attention, maybe during your meditation or just a quiet moment, perhaps while you are drinking your coffee. Make a note of the chatter and the buzz in your head. You will see how your mind picks up one thought, goes with it for a while, then drops it, picks up another one and so on.

Let me give you an example. Let's say you walk into a supermarket. Your mind is trying to remember what you had on your shopping list before leaving the house. While you walk down the vegetables aisle, you start comparing the prices and see which one is cheaper, which one is more expensive. Then you pick one kilo of potatoes and think about the recipe your mom told you about. You replay the phone conversation you had with her two days ago and try to see with your mind's eye the piece of paper where you wrote down the ingredients. Oh - parsley. Where do they keep the herbs section in this supermarket? And so on... I'm sure you got my point.

In yoga and in meditation, this is called the "monkey mind". It just jumps around from one thought to the other, just like a monkey jumps from one tree to another. The Buddhist techniques are meant to make your monkey mind slow down, take a break or quiet down. In other words, let the monkey sit in a tree and enjoy the view or eat a banana. Similarly, your mind needs to slow down and enjoy the silence.

This state of constant noise in your mind is beautifully explained in the book *The Dynamic Way of Meditation*: "Restlessness implies a state of unhappiness, a lack of satisfaction and is a manifestation of pain. The mind is not satisfied with something. It looks for something pleasurable and enjoyable. When it cannot succeed, it complains and is continually dissatisfied. This is the typical characteristic of a restless mind. But if you look into what is lacking or what the mind is anticipating, you will understand the situation and accept it as it is."

Now, many people argue that thoughts cannot be controlled and that we are helpless in front of them. There are also others - myself included - who claim that thoughts are within our control, they are what we give them permission to be and they come from deeper layers of subconsciousness. Dhiravamsa further adds: "Feeling is the language of the body and mind. If you want to understand what the body or mind is trying to convey to you, you need to watch the feeling at the point of contact. Then you will know exactly what it is talking about [...] The language of life is feeling. You come to understand what your life is communicating to you when you attend to and observe feeling."

The key is to be aware. Notice your feelings in order to make a shift in your thoughts. If you are just a slave of your thoughts, then your subconsciousness will dictate your thoughts for ever and ever. No matter how beautiful those thoughts are, wouldn't you feel more safe and confident if you knew that you have full responsibility over your mind? If you just let the mind wander, it will only repeat patterns. It will create thoughts that won't be in accordance with reality. You will start feeling unnecessary pain and sadness. You might end up drowning in depression, all because you allowed your thoughts to go wild.

The second you become aware of the thoughts that rise to the surface, you can look at them objectively. You can make different decisions and you can even change the way you think about circumstances.

Our background and our education - from family, from school, from society - plant seeds of how and what we are supposed to be thinking about. When we grow up, it doesn't come naturally for us to question these thoughts or to challenge them. Only through experience and further knowledge, as well as a thirst for getting out of our patterns will change this. I will bring up Dhiravamsa's book again, because he puts this in a very clear light, comparing our conditioning to "knots that form our conditioned patterns arising from social rules and our tendency to conform to social rules. If we have negative feelings, we should look closer at them, they are always connected with some idea or expectation in our mind. On recognizing the cause, we can let it go."

Firstly, begin noticing your thoughts, one by one. Then you will have to make a note of what triggers them. See if there is a pattern. Lastly and only, by trial and error, you will be able to make the shift. This three-step process is useful when it comes to the negative beliefs that are ingrained into our personality because we were instructed to do so.

By noticing some of the thoughts and questioning where they come from, we can dig into them layer after layer ("why did I refuse to buy that dress?" - because it was too expensive - because I was taught not to spend money on useless things - because my parents never bought expensive clothes for themselves - because it would make me feel guilty if my parents ask me how much it cost etc.).

As soon as you start seeing bothering thoughts, you will start connecting them to the way you feel. All the moods and the emotional carousel that you go through during the day is strictly connected to your thoughts. If you want to feel better, all you have to do is change your thoughts. In other words, *you* have the power. Isn't that awesome?

The only obstacle that sits between your current state and your happiness is the work you need to do on yourself and on your way of thinking.

All emotions have their roots in our minds. Even when we are not aware of the specific thought, we need to look closer and pay attention. There might be times when we don't really know why we feel a certain way and those are the moments when we need to make an additional effort to see what is going on.

I'll tell you a story that happened to me recently. One morning I woke up with a knot in my stomach. I figured it might be something I had eaten the previous day, so didn't really pay attention. I was angry at everyone around me and every little thing put me on the edge. It's not my digestion, I told myself. I realised it was something I needed to discover. I accepted the challenge because I knew that since the pain in my stomach didn't go away, it was only me that could actually do whatever was needed to make it go away.

I sat down and wrote on paper what the major concerns were I had at that particular time. I sat through guided meditations. I relaxed myself to a point where I could listen closely to what my inner voice was saying. I noticed I kept thinking "I will finish my book", "I will receive the design of my cover", "I will finally do what I love". The knot got tighter and tighter.

So, I tried an experiment. I started consciously telling myself, "you will not be able to finish it on time", "you will not be able to reach that deadline", "you will fail". And you know what happened? My stomach would relax. I became more and more able to breathe. My body was used to the comfort zone of the negative inner chatter. This was one of my beliefs about myself, that I wasn't capable of finalising my work on time, that I wasn't going to be able to do my work.

My body was instantly relaxing when my thoughts would reassure it that I would not succeed. When my mind dared to see the success on the other hand, my body revealed the fear. It released the well-hidden beast from its cage. It made me feel sick so that I would stop thinking about success and get back into convincing myself that I wouldn't make it. Becoming aware of it just made it easier to work through the pain. Through meditation I regained my balance. My stomach got back to normal too.

The meaning of this story is that one's level of awareness can make miracles. If you're not aware, your mind will draw you to your safe zone and you will want to protect yourself with thoughts that give you peace of mind.

Even when not fully articulated, thoughts still hold a major power over our feelings and our body sensations. Mind and body are closely connected in so many ways. Just think about the principles of yoga and meditation. We make efforts to look into our minds by keeping our body still in meditation. We look at our body as we stretch it and maintain a balance through yoga by keeping our mind still.

Different emotions are reflected in different parts of the body. In terms of centres of energy, these parts are chakras, where energy is stored and channelled through to the associated organs. The more you sit down and write about them, the closer you get to the bottom of them.

One of my favourite exercises that always helps me in difficult times is one that was initially suggested to me by my therapist when I was going to sessions to get over my panic attack. I would call it "STaF exercise" (Situations, Thoughts and Feelings). This can be practiced every day or whenever you feel the need to make sense of the mess inside of you (find more details in chapter 3).

For instance, you might notice that even though you receive a piece of good news, like a promotion or winning a car in the lottery, you might surprise yourself with a sad or worried mood, due to the workload that comes with the new job role or the price of fuel for the new car. It is perfectly normal to have conflicting feelings in certain situations. Not everything is black and white around us. In fact, most things have both good and bad sides. By definition, our humanity makes us indecisive and controversial.

With practice, you will be able to see a red flag whenever a specific thought will make you feel uncomfortable. This exercise might also help you when you need to make up your mind about a decision that rationally makes sense but doesn't feel right. Just write it down, untangle the thoughts and the feelings related to it.

Since we are covering the aspect of awareness in this chapter, it would be reckless not to talk about meditation. I've already told you how meditation has helped me settle my thoughts and figure out what was bothering me. After all, this is the purpose of meditation, to make us more aware of the present moment, to make our mind more connected to now rather than overthinking the past or being concerned about the future.

The secret to awareness is to stay connected to breath. By being aware and present in the moment, by focusing on our breathing, we are grounded and we stay connected with ourselves. We can simply meditate and keep a notebook and a pen close to us. As soon as the buzz calms down, we can start writing to make sense of the mess.

Writing with awareness is like meditating with the guidance of paper. Of course, you might as well perform any other activities that keep you mindful, but the main point is to be comfortable and stay with the mind. Only a person who is not confident and who is scared of their own thoughts keeps themselves busy all the time. Meditation, or any other activity completed mindfully, ties you and your thoughts together. You are meant to be best friends with your mind. You live together all your life and there is no escape from that. If you are enemies with it, you need to come to peace at once. Sooner or later, you will come to realise the true power of the mind.

For instance, Rachel Kelly, author of *Walking on Sunshine: 52 Small Steps to Happiness* tells the story of her favourite mindful activity: washing her hands. Whenever she feels stressed, she takes a break, runs to the bathroom and washes her hands. This brings her to the present moment, to feeling the touch of the water on her hands, watching the bubbles that start to form from the soap, the sound of the splashing water from the tap to the sink. There is mindfulness in each and every small activity.

How does it work?

- Choose one mundane activity that you can do anytime and that is included in your daily routine. It could be brushing your teeth, washing the dishes or brushing your hair.

- Write down the sensations and feelings associated with this action in order to engrave it into your memory.

- Take a break from a situation that proves to be stressful (for instance, step out of a meeting at work or excuse yourself from a family dinner) to go and find your presence. Reconnect with yourself every single time by doing this one activity by choice.

- If you chose an action you include in your routine, take advantage of those few moments to stay grounded and bring your mind back to reality.

When it comes to writing in relation to mindfulness, Rachel Kelly replied in the interview she offered me for this book that, "writing requires focus to think clearly and express yourself clearly."

Another practice that you might find useful to bring you back to the present moment and become aware of your feelings is mind-mapping.

We've already agreed that our minds are chaotic. We therefore agree that from time to time we need to bring some structure to the mind. And we can also agree that people are very different. Some people might prefer a more pragmatic approach, with a bit more structure and organisation. The analytical types will most likely find this tool the most useful.

Mind-mapping structures feelings in layers, from central to peripheric. The main feeling, or what is usually called the "top of mind" will be the thought that first pops into our mind when mentioning a situation or a person. This will trigger one set of emotions. Potentially under each feeling there are additional whys and whats and hows that will uncover secondary emotions. This is, as you can notice, another way of digging deeper into the layers of feelings that overwhelm us at any one point in time.

Most of the time, you might have trouble noticing a predominant thought. You can start from the situation itself as an objective "top of mind". Then place your thoughts in a circular mode on the same level. As long as it allows you to dig deeper into your mind, you can make this organisation work in your own way.

All the previous exercises discussed in this chapter (STaF, mindfulness or mind-mapping) have the power of revealing patterns and limiting beliefs that prevent us from developing unbiased emotions and judgements. It is our choice to break the cycle and the repetitive model, even if that means getting out of our comfort zone.

What we need to keep in mind is that oppositional feelings are ok and that it is our duty to explore where each side of the coin comes from. Just make sure you are always aware of what is inside of you, check in with yourself every time and don't ignore your feelings. Don't run away from terrifying emotions, just work with them and through them, crack them open into a million pieces to see what's at the bottom of it all.

In time, when you know what triggers your own negative behaviours, you will know how to choose and control, divide and conquer.

Much of this chapter has been dedicated to negative feelings, but only for the purpose of making the point that these can be changed to positive ones. When it comes to positive feelings, being aware is even more important as this is where our happiness and joy lays. Manifesting positivity in writing will always be in your favour, as it will help you visualise your happiness.

Take for instance the action of writing down your goals. By planning and giving a structure to your objectives, it will raise your excitement, make you accountable for your tasks, help you evaluate and keep track of your goals. Creating a list of goals will make you aware of what you truly want. You will be able to break down your big goals into smaller goals and tasks, which will make them more achievable. Writing about what makes you excited and happy will undoubtedly raise your spirits.

Another benefit sits on the spiritual side. By manifesting the universal power through putting your desires out there, you attract what your heart really wants. Writing it down is the commitment you take in making anything in your power. This is the way you co-create the path to your goals with the Universe.

Remember that the beauty of it all is to stay aware of your feelings. And what better way of staying in the present moment is there than writing? Write your negative thoughts, write your positive thoughts. Make a habit out of writing down your thoughts. It will not be easy at the beginning, especially if you are not used to expressing your feelings and formulating thoughts into words. Be prepared when you dive into this practice, as you might be scared of what you discover.

Keep writing periodically. Don't make writing a burden, but keep it consistent, as practice builds with time and so does your awareness.

Write when you need to release the pain.

Write when you feel that negative emotions are overwhelming your mind like the clouds do the sky.

Write when you feel happy or sad after receiving news.

Write to check in with your inner critic and your best friend - your mind - before you make a decision.

Write when you want to plan and list your goals.

Write when you feel the most need to manifest positivity, to bring all the good feelings to the surface of your awareness, to enjoy them and to keep them in your memory.

Write in a list on three columns.

Write in a mind-map.

Write with the confidence and trust that you are one step closer to understanding your feelings. This will help you. It will heal you.

CHAPTER 5

Writing to plan goals

Making plans is what keeps us all going. Be it planning for the next holiday or for your business on a long term, our excitement rises by thinking about what the future will be like.

It's true, we can easily get lost in contemplating the future. We can forget to enjoy the present moment, but if we go back and remember what we have just discussed in the previous chapter, we now have the tools to come back and be aware, to be grounded and stay with the feelings and sensations in our bodies.

Nevertheless, planning has its own advantages. What is important to keep in mind is to enjoy the journey instead of holding our breath for the future. Success is not an end goal that we need to look up to. Success is climbing the ladder and taking it step by step. If it happens overnight, there will be no fulfilment, just as there will be no journey to remember, no memories, no lessons. Make sure you plan realistically and within an achievable timeline. This is something I will come back to later in this chapter.

When you think about your goals, you must imagine a road that takes you to that objective. But that road will not magically unfold in front of you. Instead, you need to plan and take it step by step.

I've always been a list maker. Everyone around me knows I love making lists. I make lists for all sorts of things. When I was young, I used to make lists of songs I would hear in a day, lists of movies I wanted to watch, lists of books I wanted to read over the summer vacation. Thinking back, I can attribute my addiction for lists to a couple of sources.

Firstly, rationalisation had been engraved into my personality since an early age by my dad. He is an engineer. Maths has always been his passion, so he was truly happy to see I was loving it too. And I did, up until high school. My dad would help me with my homework during primary school. I got good grades and went to maths competitions. It must have been during those years that my analytical senses developed. I moulded my personality to make decisions based on reasons rather than emotions. My passion for maths vanished in high school. Perhaps I could blame the teacher but it was probably also due to my true passion for creativity that was starting to creep up again. So listing arguments, considering pros and cons, making lists became part of my own process.

Secondly, it is something I have also inherited from my mom. She loves making lists. She always writes things down, has post-its all over the place, and reminds me and my dad about our tasks or shopping duties all the time. Growing up with this has undoubtedly influenced me. It has made me write things down whenever I have to remember things.

All in all, lists have been something I've always been passionate about. Now I see how I benefit from them and so I'm sharing these stories.

When you put down a to-do list, you make a commitment. You confide your intentions to that piece of paper (or your Google calendar or phone app) and you commit to take action. You hold yourself accountable for what you have planned. Besides, whenever you think of a future goal that you want to achieve, you don't necessarily think about how to get there. It's only when you start planning and making a list that you gain structure to your thoughts about what you need to do in order to get to that end result.

Writing down your goals and listing them on paper gives you an overview for your near-future plans as well as your long-term desires. You know these goals can change through time, but at the same time you are aware that you have something to look forward to.

As professor Sonja Lyubomirsky explains in her *How of Happiness*: "Because writing is highly structured, systematic and rule-bound, it prompts you to organise, integrate and analyse your thoughts in a way that would be difficult to do if you were just fantasizing in your head. So, writing about your goals helps you put your thoughts together in a coherent manner, allowing you to find meaning in your life experiences. Writing about your dreams also gives you an opportunity to learn about yourself, to better understand your priorities, your emotions and your motives, your identity, who you really are and what's in your heart."

Coming back to one of my childhood memories, I remember whenever my parents would plan a holiday - be it a road trip or a vacation in the mountains, I would immediately start making lists of what I would pack with me and what I would need to do before I left. It was exciting. It kept me thinking about all the preparations for my upcoming holiday. Lists can give you something to look forward to, they can make things happen.

If you're thinking "OK, what if I don't have any specific goals right now?", I will tell you a secret: you do have a goal. Maybe even more than one. You just need clarity of what that goal is. If you imagine yourself in five years' time, how do you see yourself? Put down the book for a couple of minutes, close your eyes and visualise your future self five years from now.

I'm going to assume you've done just that, so now grab pen and paper and write down how you visualised yourself. Or turn to the end of the book where you have some space for this. Where are you living, what do you do for a living, what are your passions, who do you live with, how do you spend your day? Just picture it with your mind's eye. It will make it seem more real. You basically see yourself in your own shoes, doing the things you desire to do and it suddenly becomes achievable. You know it is possible because you've just seen yourself doing it in the future. Isn't it great?

If you are still struggling with this visualisation exercise, don't give up. Make sure you are in a safe, quiet place, that you are not distracted, that you are not sleepy and that you are not in a rush. Repeat the exercise, close your eyes and relax. Take a couple of deep breaths and start imagining. Picture the date on the calendar. It's five years from today. Where are you? How are you?

Another great way to release the goals that are trapped in your subconscious is meditation. You can try either silent meditation or guided meditation. Visualisation during meditation takes you to even deeper layers of your mind, where you can explore what you truly want.

Meditation can also guide you through setting your intentions and visualising yourself accomplishing that goal. Let me tell you a story that happened earlier during the year when I was writing this book. During my morning meditation practice, I once visualised myself standing on a stage, giving a speech to a crowd. It had been something I had always wanted to do despite all the scary feelings associated with it. Guess what? Two weeks later, while I was attending an event, I offered to speak on stage, right then and there. Many other people were willing to take the mic that night, but I was chosen to go up there and give a talk for 10 minutes. It was only a few days after that I connected my meditation visualisation to what had happened. I knew then how powerful visualisation can be. My latest visualisation is picturing myself on the tube while the passenger across from me is reading my book. And I know it will happen.

Planning for your goals can sometimes be confusing and overwhelming. You might as well think, "But I have so many goals, which ones do I focus on?". You are of course the best person to identify and choose, what I call, *pain points* in your own life. You can address this with a coach or mentor in case you feel you need clarity for your priorities. They are qualified to offer you the tools you need to re-order your focus for the near future. However, what you need to keep in mind is that once you start working and planning for reaching a goal in one area of your life, all the other aspects of your life will be influenced.

As soon as you are clear about your objectives and the dream life you are working towards, you can start planning for it. You can start by writing down a list of actions you are able to start implementing at once. This will kick off your plan of action.

You may think this sounds too pretentious and that you are not ready to create a plan of action. You won't even believe how easy it is to create it. It is even easier to follow it once you know what to do step by step. But first thing's first. What is a plan of action? It is a list of things you need to do in order to achieve your goal. When you have a goal, you know what the end result is. You know how it looks like and what it is that you are working towards. It's refreshing to see and you become more anxious to get there. When you write down your goals, it is like you are already committing to make it happen. Your goal is your destination. All you have to do is take the journey to your destination now.

Remember those maths problems from school? (Yeah, I know, I secretly brought up maths again). You are now in point A, which is your starting point or your departure. Your goal is point B. You don't need to calculate the speed or the distance, all you have to do is to create the journey. Plan the steps you need to take in order to get from A to B. Think of it as a map for your trip. This is your action plan.

When you create your plan and you start writing it down, it will become more and more realistic. What I would like you to keep in mind when you write down your action plan are the following three pieces of advice:

- **Be flexible** - don't get angry if it doesn't turn out the way you want it to. We can't always control the end result of our actions and we can certainly not control the circumstances and the factors that influence these actions. Always have alternative options in mind, stay flexible in the roads you are taking in your journey and you will still reach that goal; however, don't be surprised if sometimes even the goal changes along the way. Stay open-minded. Enjoy it.

- **Be resourceful** - when you plan your actions, always think about resources, who can help you, where you can find support and where you need to outsource. Creativity will get you a long way and finding unexpected solutions will pay off when you start getting closer and closer to your objective.

- **Don't give up** - having a goal and a plan of action will not spare you the failures and obstacles along the way. It's all in you and how much you want to reach the destination. This is in fact the beauty of the journey. You have a goal, but the lessons and the stories you collect along the way will be your biggest asset.

Now that you have decided what your goal is and you've established your plan of action, it's time to get to work. When you start planning, it will help if you break down your big goal into smaller objectives. These will be the milestones of your journey that will give you a sense of accomplishment. They will make you feel that you are moving forward, and you are moving forward.

Each milestone will have bullet points translated into actionable items that will take you step by step through your journey. It is up to you whatever works best. You can plan for monthly sub-goals, but I would personally recommend breaking it down into weekly goals, or even into daily steps. It will feel smoother. It will move you every day in the right direction. When you are focusing on a goal, it is important to sense your evolution.

Another very important part of your action plan is the timeline. This is where most people lose track of their goals. It's easy to set up goals and launch them in your head like you would tell your wish to the little goldfish, but it is more realistic and believable if you set a goal by a specific date. For instance, you want to be able to run 10k by the end of April. Or you want to earn X amount of money by the 1st February. Always set up deadlines for your goals and stick to them. Then when you break them down into actions, set closer deadlines. Work it out backwards, with the end goal in mind. What you need to do tomorrow, what you need to do by the end of the week, then next month and so on. Write it down in colours, draw tables or make a diagram. Whichever option works for you, find your motivation in it and do it.

Once you have a clear timeline, with deadlines and milestones, you need to write it down and make sure you follow it. Your first level of commitment is to the paper and to yourself, but you may find it more motivating if you hand the paper to a friend or even a coach that will hold you accountable for your promised actions. Make it clear what the non-negotiables for your action plan are and stay determined.

Since I've always been passionate about making lists, I can confess that one of the most satisfying things about a list is the moment when you cross something off it. If you are not used to making lists, next time you head to the supermarket, prepare a list of groceries and any other items you need to buy for the household. Then when you come back home, cross everything you have bought off the list. You have to admit, it's pretty satisfying.

When it comes to your action plan, the secret is to plan small tasks and include them in your daily routine. Write down even the small things that make up part of your schedule, the tasks that you know there is no way you won't do. This will help you in your endeavour to cross things off your list. If you are not used to lists, start small. Write down "brush teeth" and at the end of the day I guarantee there will be something to cross off your list.

As I have already mentioned, staying flexible is crucial. Make sure you don't get frustrated if you don't cross everything off your list on the day. Review the list. Did you plan for more than you had time for? Did you make a timeline? Did you include both your routine and your steps for the goal? Make sure to not stretch yourself too much, being frustrated doesn't really help you.

This is actually the way to make your list your best friend. Many people end up hating lists because they become slaves of their own lists. It shouldn't be that way. Lists are meant to be your support. It is in your power to make the list work for you. Make it work in your favour and be friends with it. Make the list actionable. Break it down into small steps so that whenever you look at it, you don't start panicking. Instead, feel the urge to take action and start doing the things from the list. That's the whole purpose after all, right? If you put down difficult items or activities that require multiple steps, it will be more difficult to keep up with it. It will require more time before you can actually cross it off the list. So it is all in your control to make it easy and helpful instead of turning it into a nightmare.

I keep coming back to the flexibility piece of advice, as this is really important for your mental state and motivation. I can't stress enough how important it is to be open-minded. When things don't go as you have imagined, change the actions you had planned or change your goal if it doesn't benefit you anymore. Staying stubborn will not do you any good. Reorder your priorities, your tasks, your deadlines. Make it achievable. Once again, it is in your power to do all this.

If you keep in mind the end result that you want to achieve, that goal that you have written down and committed to, you will start seeing new perspectives along the way. If something doesn't work out, your mind will start creating solutions. You might even get to see your planned actions in a fresh light.

Let's take an example. When I was in university, one of my goals was to study abroad. I had no idea how to get there and what I needed to do. I first applied for a scholarship in Germany to do my master's. I was rejected because I didn't speak the language and they didn't have any courses in English. I then found out about exchange programmes for students, but in order to apply for one I had to be enrolled in a master's program in my own country. I therefore did that and studied for one year in Romania, while applying for Erasmus and creating all the necessary documents for it. I was eventually accepted to study abroad for one semester in the second year of my master's. Off I went to Helsinki for six months. You see, I achieved my goal to study abroad, but when my first action plan failed, I was flexible and changed my approach.

Now that you have an action plan that guides you towards your goal, you need to keep track of what you are doing. The best and most reliable way would be to keep a journal of your plan and what you are achieving on a daily or weekly basis. Put down what small steps you have taken, what you have learned, what you changed or how you adapted your approach. Keep track of the feedback you get and the way it makes you feel. Keep track of the small victories with each and every milestone that you reach.

Writing it down will make it easier to return and review your actions. Learning from mistakes, improving, repeating processes that worked out, adjusting or implementing the knowledge you've once gained will be invaluable. Keeping it in writing will be more reliable than your memory and you can even use colour coding in order to mark down positives and negatives.

In addition to that, tell someone you trust about what you're doing. Make sure you choose someone to confide in that won't judge you or envy you along the way. If you feel you are not as close as this with any member of your family or friends, just get yourself a coach and make your journey easier.

Last but not least, give the Universe some credit. Be thankful to the unknown ways that the Universe has and let it do its magic. Remember at the beginning of the chapter when we were talking about setting intentions and visualisation? Once you launch your objectives and desires . into the Universe, it will contribute to your efforts. It's the Law of Attraction. It doesn't hurt to trust a greater power.

Keeping track of the steps you are taking will make it super easy to spot your progress and stay on the right path. If you have a journal where you have written down your goals and the steps, the first sign of progress will be crossing off the list what you complete.

It's not enough to just keep track and see the progress. I know I am repeating myself, but it is all about enjoying the journey. So take time to acknowledge your victories. Reward yourself. Take care of yourself. It's essential to keep your self-esteem and self-confidence high.

Be continuously grateful for all your achievements, no matter how big or small they are. Perhaps you will find it motivating if you keep a gratitude journal. You can write in it every evening and thank the Universe for three things that have happened during the day. Or you can practice it in the morning. You don't even have to do it daily if you don't feel it will benefit you. Sometimes repeating a task every day can make it less enjoyable and those tasks turn into burdens. If you feel like you are not enjoying writing in your gratitude journal, make it less regular, write weekly or whenever you feel the need. However, it's important to stay on the side of achievement. Be grateful for everything that comes your way.

The last point I am going to touch on is time. You need to be very careful when you organise your most precious asset, which is your time. That is why you need a timeline, an overview of the planned actions and when they can be completed by. Make sure you keep your timeline clear and write it down in your agenda. Keep it with you at all times; a notebook that can fit in your purse or your backpack, so that you are always sure to have it with you.

Personally, I work best with agendas, but as we live in a constantly growing digital world, agendas and written schedules are now replaced by mobile apps and digital calendars. Choose the one that fits you the best and that you feel most comfortable with. Not as comfortable as to forget about it, but enough to remind you about your meetings, your tasks and your plans.

In the same way you schedule blocks of time in your calendar for meetings or other social activities, make sure to block time for taking care of yourself or for your work.

Leave flexibility for spontaneous decisions, but stay on top of your planned actions all the time.

You might learn this from trial and error, but I will just raise this flag now. You need to set yourself some realistic deadlines. Instead of scheduling tight deadlines full of intense work, make sure you can accomplish your sub-goal in the timeline you settled for. Don't leave it too late. You want to feel like you are taking steps towards your goal every day. Just remember, don't burnout. It's better and more effective if you take small but constant steps towards the end goal. Feel free to test it, keep track of it and see the difference. Then you can choose your own style for delivering your action plan.

Exercise 1

Grab a pen and a piece of paper and sit in a relaxed mood. Visualise yourself in five years' time. Write down what comes up in your visualisation. This will give you an idea of your areas of interest and the immediate goals that really matter to you. Stay with your visualisation and keep your pen going on the paper. Compared to where you are now, what would you need in order to get to your ideal self in five years? Write the goals, then start breaking it down into sub-goals and then further into actionable items. You might realise that you can achieve that lifestyle sooner than in five years. What a revelation that would be! All you have to do now is to take action according to your plan.

Exercise 2

Make a list of the things you know you have to do in the next month. Break it down and put deadlines next to each action that you need to take. Later on, return to your list and cross off the items that have been fulfilled. Thank yourself, the Universe and whoever else supported you during this time.

CHAPTER 6

Writing to share

Most of the time when we think about healing we might see it as something shameful, something that we wouldn't want to share with anyone around us. When we go through tough times, we tend to put up walls to not let others see what we are truly experiencing. We might lie to ourselves saying that it comes from a desire of protecting our loved ones from worrying about us. Most likely it comes from a place of embarrassment and fear to be judged.

The worst part is that we end up lying to ourselves. If we don't go through the healing process, no matter how often we repeat "everything is ok" we will reach a point when things will surface and all the accumulated feelings will be more difficult to cope with. No matter how much we hide our pain and go home to cry into our pillows, emotions will win in the end.

Now I'm not saying to start being miserable whenever you go out with your friends. I'm just saying: be honest! Tell your friends what is bothering you. Speak to your family. Speak to a specialised counsellor, therapist or coach. It is easier to go through painful times when you have someone by your side.

It's the same with writing. Yes, you can write and write in order to let it all out and let it go. You can use any of the exercises from the previous chapters to do that and gain tremendous results, but in the same way embarrassment and fear of judgement seem to keep us from talking to the people around us about our problems. At that point, we can hesitate to share our written thoughts.

Writing has this beautiful effect of giving you the opportunity to express yourself without needing an audience or a receptor, you can just go ahead and write it all on paper and then throw it away or burn it. Paper is not judgemental. Paper doesn't take sides and doesn't make you feel bad. You don't have to censor your words. You can just allow the flow of thought to be reflected on paper.

Journaling is probably the best example of what writing for self really means. In my teenage years when I used to keep a journal, I couldn't afford buying one with a lock, so instead I would use tape to secure its covers (as if...). That is, until I found another way to keep my thoughts private from the curious eyes of my parents. I started writing in foreign languages, either English or Spanish. The fear of my mom and dad knowing about my school crush and then mocking me or going to tell him...

When we grow up, this fear of being judged continues, it is already instilled in us and we just take it to the next level. We might still use journaling with the idea of pouring our souls on paper knowing that our confident will be there the next day too, never raising eyebrows no matter what we say or do or write.

How about trying to overcome this barrier? Writing is therapeutic either way, but did you know that you can use it not only for yourself, but also for sharing? The simple act of writing is one stage of the healing process. The transformation happens with the next actions taken with that piece of paper.

This is indeed a highly controversial topic, and perhaps not yet supported by academic research, but from experience, there is something to it. Bear with me.

As discussed in previous chapters, the first step in healing is grief and acceptance. Only after that can you start dealing with the pain internally and start to explore the emotions in writing, figuring it all out. Well, let me tell you there is an optional third part of that which involves you sharing some of your writing. Whether it is a compliment or a complaint, we need to force ourselves to step out of our comfort zone. Speak up or write it out, but don't leave it like that.

Now this is not applicable for any type of communication. Society's unwritten rules makes us be polite, but sometimes being polite can end up with us lying to each other. We don't really know how to express the truth and that supresses our right to speak. We fear bothering the other person or offending them if we pay a compliment. We fear. We actually overthink it so much that we end up being scared. Instead of sending a text message saying "Sorry", we end up saying nothing. Or instead of thanking someone for a nice gesture over email, we just ignore it.

How about when someone hurts us? Why not tell them in writing what we feel? Letters were once the most popular way to do this. People were not very generous in information, but boy did they make it sound fancy on paper. Choosing our words carefully should not be part of the equation, as all we need to do is to give a voice to what we are truly feeling. Because if we ruminate over it, we take too long and in the end give up writing and give up sending a letter at all.

Letters can hold powerful meaning. It's the handwriting that holds the magic. Throughout history, war was declared through letters. Love and romance would build and break in letters. All types of news were delivered in the written word. When there was something bothering the king or the queen, they would send a letter to complain or sign a deal with their rivals. You get the point. Letters are powerful.

When used in therapeutic purposes, letters get to be written and addressed to someone who hurt us, but they may or may not be sent. This is the choice of the writer.

Imagine this exercise: you are invited to write a letter to someone who has acted in a wrongful way to you. Write everything that has bothered you and how it made you feel. If it was a repeated interaction with the same result, write to clear things up about how you felt every single time and what each of their reactions and words made you feel. Be clear and specific. Don't censor yourself. See it as your time to share your side of the story.

This is a very powerful technique or exercise to use frequently if you are an introvert. As far as I am concerned, I don't like fighting. If there is anything that I really dislike and try to avoid it is arguing with someone. Raising my voice and addressing words that we might later regret are the types of interactions that make me feel uncomfortable. So, when I would get caught in the middle of a fight and the other person would start shouting, I would shut up. Staying quiet would give them the space to eliminate all their anger, which may not even have anything to do with me, but it would inevitably affect me emotionally and make me keep all my emotions to myself. I knew that if I'd opened my mouth to speak, my opinions wouldn't be met with reason, but with rejection and further shouting and blame. All this would just pile up inside of me and even if I did my fair share of crying, it would still not mean enough of a release.

It is all these emotions that pile up inside of us that make it difficult to heal. Therefore, if we don't get the chance to tell the other person in words our side of the story, we still have an opportunity to do it in writing.

Personally, I prefer sharing whatever I write about a certain relationship or former partner, because I feel it benefits both of us. I get to write it down and release all the emotions related to those thoughts and speak my mind. He gets to hear my side of the story and hopefully learn a lesson on what not to do in the future and how not to treat another woman. In fact, this is a service that is meant to be done for the benefit of all womankind.

In today's modern world, we rarely speak through letters anymore. It's too bad, but it is what it is, and we need to keep up with digitised forms of communication. On the bright side, we have more means to share our side of the story. It's not dependent on a horse ride anymore.

If you do end up deciding that your story needs to be put out in the world, then by all means, make it happen! The world we are living in encourages us to shut up and replicate behaviours that we see around us. Deficient leaders rule the world. The masses are encouraged to just follow. But we all have a voice. It is our duty to speak up. So, if you do feel ready to share your story, do it! Write it and share it with everyone!

Now I am not saying to point fingers, shame other people in public or practice dissemination of rumours. I'm saying share your story. Your feelings, your learnings, your truth. You never know who you will end up helping or inspiring with your story. Because there is only one *you* in the world and your story is unique.

What we need to do is to just get out of our own heads and see it all from an objective perspective. I'm sure your mind can produce so many excuses as to why you need to keep your story to yourself, but if you take a step back and look at it from an outside point of view you will start seeing the reasons why you should share it.

Thank the Universe for technology. We can now reach thousands of people around the world online. Take bloggers for example. It is so easy to create a blog for free that you can use as a platform to tell your stories to the world.

My story with blogging started when I was going through a very dynamic stage of my life in terms of dating. I felt that all that was happening to me on the dating front was worth sharing with the whole world, if not for anything else at least for a good laugh. Most of all I felt it was my duty to warn the women out there about the douchebags running free on the streets or hiding under the good guy's mask. And I took this responsibility very seriously. I didn't consider myself an expert in dating, far from being it. However, I attracted so many funny, painful, eventful experiences in my life when it came to dating that it was therapy for me to write about it. It was also a way to keep a record and make mental notes on what to do, what not to do, what to avoid in the future. Back then, it was so important to break patterns and my only rule was "the more different, the better". I had no idea why I was attracting all these negative stories, but that's for another chapter.

Blogging gave me a sense of having a voice. It allowed me to share my stories and get feedback and that was really empowering. Writing your story contributes to your life in so many ways. The power of storytelling can make a huge impact and even change lives.

When we recall a memory and start writing it down or telling it to someone else, there are certain details that stick with us. Depending on our emotional state, we either remember the happy details of the story or the side that made us sad. Long term, it is very subjective what part our mind will remember, based on the intensity of the emotions and sensations that we've lived at that particular time. A happy moment that thrilled us when it happened will always be a happy memory. An event that made us feel hurt or upset might bring us the same sensations when we recall it. If we go through healing we will be able to see the event just as it was, an event that has come and gone. And whenever we will bring it to our mind, it will be just a memory without giving us any more pain.

Most important of all, stories are to be told. And we all have plenty of stories to share. We might be more inclined to share them or to keep them to ourselves, but we all have stories. One person can live an eventful day in their life, full of exciting things and encounters and they might think "who would want to hear it", whereas there are people who love storytelling and can transform a dull regular morning into the best story you've ever heard or read. You might be thinking it is down to the talent and the creativity of the storyteller to make a story as appealing to others as possible, but let me tell you something. It is in fact the joy of the story teller when they live that moment, be it an absolutely amazing day or the most boring morning.

What is it we can learn from this? Well, once we get past the pain, we get to see the lesson, and that's the most valuable thing and that's what needs to be shared.

All experiences, either good or bad, offer us a lesson. By sharing it, we get to at least hope that someone else will not repeat our own mistakes. Or on the contrary, if the outcome is a positive one, that they follow our steps and get to a similar good result. As foolish as this sounds, we somehow expect different results when we act the same way or follow the same pattern of thought and action.

That is why we end up reading literature that resonates with our state of mind, only to find out that the writers themselves have written it in much the same state of mind. There's something universal about stories then.

Take for example some of the most famous writers. They have all ended up putting their passion into writing and creating characters that would express how they really felt. It was their way of self-therapy and self-expression.

Making a note here, creative writing can be, but doesn't have to be, therapeutic. The true healing happens in the midst of expressive writing, when we focus on the exact emotions associated with our thoughts, which are based on real situations. Besides, creativity doesn't always come easily to everyone, however, the possibility of discipline in writing and the possibility of emotion generally is more widely spread among human beings.

Studies show that one in four people go through a mental health problem at least once during their life. I bet they're not all fiction writers. What they do have handy however, is a pen and paper and their will to explore their innermost thoughts and feelings. Sharing your story and your struggle can have such an impact and change someone's life without even realising it.

Sharing our story with the world is first and foremost a way to relieve our own anxiety. Emotions that are left unexpressed build up inside of us and, just like a snowball, they become bigger and bigger. Then, just like that snowball, they hit a wall and explode. Or if you'd like, you can imagine the emotions building up inside you like a balloon that inflates and inflates and in the end pops. Your emotions will eventually pop too if you don't remove the pressure and the accumulated air. If you start sharing, you will get your issues out of your mind.

Another reason to write and share is that you get to break a barrier. You get to step out of your comfort zone. And when your comfort zone is the one that doesn't allow you to express your concerns and your opinions then that is something that you will definitely need to be looking to break. It takes a lot of courage to be able to put yourself out there. Many people don't find the courage required, so they remain quiet. Yet instead of relieving their anxiety, they become more and more anxious.

Just imagine the relief when your fear is overcome! There will be nothing unbeatable anymore. You are a hero. Your intake on life switches immediately. You become free of the anxiety of sharing your story and your self-esteem improves. It takes little steps to get there, but Rome wasn't built in a day.

Once you do this, you might even be surprised to see that you are not alone. And this is yet another reason why sharing stories is such a powerful healing technique. Having gone through similar experiences gives people a sense of community. They all have something in common, but they won't be aware of it unless they share it. People need to know they are not alone.

For instance, whenever I used to find myself in a position of going through a break up, I would go on Google and search for "10 ways to get over a break up" and then ended up reading article after article about ways to move on. The truth was however, it wasn't about the how to get over the break-up that helped me. Not really. It was by reading these stories that I related to the ones who had written them. They made me realise that I wasn't the only one who had gone through heartbreak. I thought to myself, *if all these other people have survived going through a heartbreak, then I will too.*

If you are in the millennials' generation, you might remember forums, which used to build up communities around a specific passion or hobby. If some social networks today are more for showing off than supporting, forums back in the days were about sharing and making you proud that you were part of that community. It was like being part of a fan club, even it was just talking about the wonders of fixing gardening tools. The whole point was to make sure we got to share stories, build up relationships and belong to a community. We now have even more online communities and sharing joy or sharing sorrows brings us closer and makes us all feel surrounded by people who understand us and are part of the same community.

To be honest with you, that was my reason behind creating the story-sharing platform TheGuyThat. It came from a need to tell stories that would not require a lesson or a conclusion. Just tell the story, share it as it is, leave it anonymous and feel relieved. It is meant to be a safe place where one can express herself about the guy that impacted her life, either in a positive or a negative way. Just like speaking and sharing stories with their girlfriends, the women who would get to write their stories would feel relieved. Then I received requests from men wanting to express their feelings who had been holding them back from recovering after a break up. So we all have a desire to share our stories.

Once again, you can try to think about this as an exercise. Keep a pen and a piece of paper close by. Think about an unpleasant moment in your life and the person who made you feel that way. If you had the opportunity to have them in front of you, what would you tell them? What would you share with them?

Again, this depends on how much healing has happened beforehand, but it is a way of seeing how powerful sharing can be. Would you expect the other person to react in any way? Would you expect them to apologise or at least acknowledge? Keep in mind that you are only sharing your side of the story. In their mind, as sad as it might sound, your side of the story might not trigger any thoughts. They might be so trapped in themselves that they don't really see your perspective as a valid one. So it's important to be prepared and take into account the possibilities of reaction. Better yet, don't expect any reaction. After all, you are doing yourself a favour. You are taking action as part of your own healing by letting it all out. It's not in your control what the other person chooses to do with the information afterwards.

It can potentially be seen as a selfish act, but it is necessary. You need to let it go. If you were to choose one of your ex-romantic partners, what would you tell them?

Would you write about the break-up moment? Is that all that has stayed with you? Or would you write about the beautiful happy moments you shared during the relationship?

If we want to practice by writing a letter of forgiveness to someone who has hurt us, we need to understand that we are not doing this as a favour to them, we are doing it as a favour to ourselves, to be able to forgive, let go and move on. Professor Raj Raghunathan recommends to keep this letter to ourselves unless it comes from a place where the other person will find release in it too. Otherwise, they might see it as a patronising act. It might have the reverse effect.

When I go through a break up I feel comforted by sad stories about other people's heartbreaks. I indulge in romantic dramas and I cry while listening to sad love songs. After all, I need the validation that proves love sucks. I also like to keep the good memories of past relationships, not from a point of view of hoping for a rebound, but from a space of keeping with me only the positive things and removing the bad memories. Why would I want to clutter my mind and my soul with bad memories? Besides, all bad memories can in fact be transformed into lessons.

Speaking of past memories of romantic relationships, I challenge you to another exercise. First think about it. Then write down whatever comes to mind. Can you remember your first kiss? This is usually an innocent and positive memory, but sometimes it can trigger some negative emotions if it gets to be associated with the first relationship that might have ended in a big dramatic heartbreak. Firsts are never easy, so why not cherish the memory of them, given that it the memory of them is all that is left in the end?

Now start scribbling based on this. Stay in the expressive mode and explore the feelings that come back to you when you remember your first kiss, your first love.

Stay in the therapeutic mode that raises your awareness of your feelings. Stay with the body sensations that get to be associated with these feelings. Write through them.

The difference between fictional or creative writing and expressive writing is just how we attribute the feelings. In fiction, characters become an interface between the story and the feelings transposed. Songwriters do it when writing their music. They project their feelings into a song that might tell a different story than the real situation they have been through, but in the end they want to reach the listeners with the same emotion. Fiction writers use the same technique of projecting their thoughts into characters and fake stories, but their inspiration is taken from situations that have happened to them. Writers must live a full life in order to be inspired. As much as they would like to count on their imagination only, it is by living certain experiences that veracity is given to their stories.

Whereas in expressive therapy, inspiration is right inside of us, it is our own mind, our own thoughts and our own feelings. We don't need to think about names to put to our characters. We just need to express what goes on inside.

Last but not least, writing for sharing has also a very strong social component to it. That is when our story is so powerful and impactful that it needs to ring a bell on a much higher level, not just individually, but also culturally and socially. There are cases when there is more than a lesson, it is a way to raise a red flag about things that happen.

I'm talking here about stories such as abuse or rape. Women who have gone through these kinds of trauma are ashamed to speak up. They can barely express their feelings on paper, let alone expose themselves and share their story. There are some who know how important it is to bring awareness to these sorts of events and reveal their story in order to let other women know they are not alone. They also do so to let the rest of the world know that these things happen and they can be prevented.

One story that comes to mind in this situation is a TED talk from a rape victim who delivered a powerful speech standing right next to her attacker on stage. This picture is so impactful on so many levels, from the victim who took the responsibility to talk about what had happened to her and the rapist who was her boyfriend at the time of the rape. His level of awareness is an enormous call to men. He acknowledges his act and stands tall to take in all the judgements from the outside world who points the finger to him. But he is a representative of a category that rarely get to be pointed fingers at because these stories rarely make it to the public. There is a link to the TED talk in the annex at the back of the book, but their take is that the victim and the rapist, after both going through the healing process and reconciliation, decided to raise awareness and partnered up to create a charity and community to support rape victims. Tom Stranger confesses during his speech:

"When you own something and really square up to your culpability, I do think a surprising thing can happen. It's what I call a paradox of ownership. I thought I'd buckle under the weight of responsibility. I thought my certificate of humanity would be burnt. Instead, I was offered to really own what I did," while Thordis Elva concludes, "Breaking your silence is never easy, and depending on where you are in the world, it can even be deadly to speak out about rape. I realise that even the most traumatic event of my life is still a testament to my privilege, because I can talk about it without getting ostracized, or even killed. But with that privilege of having a voice comes the responsibility of using it."

Remember this when you think you are ready. Think about the responsibility of having a voice and the stories that we can share for the world's benefit.

CHAPTER 7

Writing for self-esteem

When it comes to my personal experience with writing, I've already mentioned quite a few key moments that have shaped my journey and included pen and paper. However, I think the strongest impact has been during the times when my self-esteem hit rock bottom and I couldn't see any escape.

Writing can save a person in many ways. It has to be experienced from a truly deep place where the echoes of shattered confidence and self-worth are so painful that they need to be put on paper. It is those circumstances that shape us most and shake us to the roots. And then we know that radical change has to be made. And we most probably have no idea what kind of change or revelation we are expecting, but we definitely crave for it. Our inner self wants it so badly because it simply can't float in that feeling of self-hatred anymore.

The thing is, nobody wants to admit they have low self-esteem. In fact, could that be the first question that pops into your head right now? "How do I know I suffer from low self-esteem?" I mean, maybe you act with confidence in social circumstances, always surrounded by people, exuding strength to the outside world, but how do you feel inside? Maybe you find it easy to talk to strangers. You might even come across as arrogant in some situations. But what goes on inside of you?

Could it be that your need of always being surrounded by people and getting all the attention in the room is actually your insecurity, your attempt at validation? Could it be that your so-perceived arrogance is actually a wall that you put up in order to avoid being hurt, in order for you to hide all your fears? Could it be that you play a game of pretending that you are this amazing popular person, when in fact you go home and cry yourself to sleep or blame yourself when looking in the mirror?

Just like removing your make-up at the end of the day, people with low self-esteem give up their mask when they are at home, alone, as they start hearing the voice from inside speaking to them. "Why did you tell him this?", "How could you do that?", "You are so stupid". If all this goes on in your head the second you look at yourself in the mirror, this is a sign of low self-esteem.

Of course, it is easy to try to ignore this voice, by keeping yourself busy and never allowing a second of silence in your mind - which in itself is a red flag - but this voice will find a way to creep up into your head one way or another, either in your most intimate moments or when you're just sitting on the toilet or taking a shower.

So your judging inner voice is one of the signs, probably one of the most important, and I will come back to it later. Another sign of a lack of self-worth is holding yourself back from opportunities, from doing things you are passionate about, by letting your excuses kick in before you make a decision.

Again, always trying to be surrounded by people, never giving yourself a break out of the fear that you will actually start hearing what goes on inside your head, is a sign you are avoiding what you actually feel. Fear of your emotions means disconnection; a disruption between you and your inner self. And I'm sure you already guessed where I am getting at. If you are disconnected from yourself and you want to keep things this way, then your self-esteem is not at its highest.

I went through all the above. In high school, my inner thinking was hyper-active and I used to ruminate over all the things that I did during a day. I used to give myself hard times because of how I reacted during one of the classes or what my classmates thought or why I even glanced in the direction of my crush. I used to then play in my head scenarios in which I would do things right and then everything would be different. Yes, you can tell I was a pretty insecure teenager. My self-esteem wasn't well nourished. I actually remember how one time in my second year of high school I somehow got the phone number of my crush, that was when I had just got my first mobile phone. So I texted him one night and my text sounded something like this "I know you probably don't want anything to do with me but just wanted to wish you Merry Christmas". My heart was pounding out of my chest and I kept staring at my phone's screen for minutes in a row hating myself, wishing there was a way to reclaim my text back. The guy actually replied in the next half an hour or so with a sweet Christmas wish but I was completely insecure and I convinced myself he didn't actually mean it so I didn't get back to him. "I know you probably don't want anything to do with me" ... How much lower could my confidence go? Talk about not taking opportunities, huh?

What I am trying to point out is that once these symptoms are discovered, they need to be addressed. It's your responsibility to raise your self-worth and do something to overcome your low self-esteem. Otherwise you risk missing out on opportunities because your fear will kick in and will hold you back. You risk staying in that sense of disconnection from yourself without actually being able to distinguish between the emotions that make life so much more colourful. In fact, if you don't make your self-esteem bloom, your life risks being all black and white and you'll miss all the other colours. Your decision making will be affected because you won't be able to analyse things from the point of view of how it makes you feel. Instead you will just do what is expected of you, and what is best for the people around you instead of what is best for you.

I can go on and on here, but I guess you got the point. YOU HAVE TO DO THE WORK AND OVERCOME YOUR LOW SELF-ESTEEM. I don't mean to shout at you but tough love works sometimes. We tend to miss things even when they are screaming in our faces. If you don't do something sooner rather than later, you might end up hitting rock bottom. At least then you will know that the only way is up.

Now these fears and insecurities are not just starting to seed into your life, they have been part of your life for a long time, maybe even from your childhood. Most of the times these are triggered by one or multiple events that make such a big impact on our lives that they just make us think the worst of ourselves. These negative beliefs create our rules of life which impact the way we go through each and every day of our existence. I'm not going to dive too deep into how these rules of life become part of yourself and all the terminology behind them. Instead, if you're interested, see Melanie Fennell's book *Overcoming Low Self-Esteem*. She mentions there how the negative beliefs about ourselves are just opinions, not facts. Most probably they are based on previous experience and background. They form something that is known in cognitive behavioural therapy as the "bottom line". This represents our ingrained opinion about ourselves. In order to survive we create our own rules for living. These rules are part of who we are and how we show ourselves to the world.

As an example from my own journey, after my major breakups from important relationships in my life, I used to build up walls around my heart and hide behind them whenever I would meet someone new. My bottom line was "I am not worthy of love from a partner", therefore I had created my own rule of living that included no emotional involvement, no attachments, in order to avoid being hurt.

These were obviously some set patterns that had started developing based on repeated experiences. In order to be able to identify these patterns, you need to ask yourself why you think those things about yourself. Why do you think you are not good enough? What makes you think this? What happened in the past that made you think this about yourself? Write down the things that come out of this exercise. See what repeating events or situations made you think in a certain way. "Writing is a way of unpacking fears and looking at your assumptions and judgements, and the harsh language we use to ourselves.[...] It is a mirror and if it is used in the right way it doesn't have to be scary, it can be a friendly way to speak to yourself differently," as Rachel Kelly puts it.

Once you've gone through these - and by all means take all the time you need to complete this exercise, as it can be painful to go back in the past and unearth the situations that lowered your self-esteem - give it a read.

Then grab a new piece of paper and ask yourself "Who am I?", "What am I?", "Where am I meant to be?", "What am I meant to be?"

Try to see how your perception changes and repeat the exercise, if necessary, until you start seeing the patterns. Think of it like Allison Price, author of *Writing From The Source - Techniques for re-scripting your Life* does: "As your own counsellor, your job is to surprise yourself into an insight to which your old habits of expectation, beliefs etc. have blinded you. And I know no way of doing it for yourself except by writing."

You need to make an effort to start paying attention to your inner voice. You need to really listen to it. You can't really just let it go on and on and drag you down. And it's only in your power to stop it!

Think about a potential situation. Think about seizing a great opportunity for the job of your dreams. Picture yourself right in front of the interview room and just listen to whatever is going on in your head. Write it down. Are you encouraging yourself or are you telling yourself, "I don't know what I am doing here, I'll definitely make a fool of myself, I'm so under-qualified". This is self-doubt serving you on a gold platter exactly what you want to hear in order to avoid disappointment if this goes wrong. So you will do what is in your power to make it go wrong. Because it would get you out of your comfort zone to actually try harder. It would make you question whether you deserve it or if you are prepared for it. Darling, you will never be prepared for it, but you can do it!

Professor Kristin Neff talks about self-compassion and this inner voice that we all have as an alternate ego inside of our head. If only we could listen to what we tell ourselves! Oh dear, we wouldn't even dare to say those things to a close friend, so how come we allow ourselves to be so harsh on us? We need to speak to ourselves in the kindest and most compassionate way, like we would to a friend in need. Hell, we should speak to us like we would speak to the love of our lives.

Instead of blaming ourselves for what goes wrong, finding ourselves guilty of all the misery that surrounds us and beating ourselves up for everything we do or say, we should just let it be. Just allow actions, thoughts and words to flow and trust them. For this, you need to be in full connection with yourself, being confident and fearless. You have to be confident enough to allow yourself to be less than perfect because that is ok. Thriving for perfectionism is most of the times hurtful because we put ourselves under pressure and become anxious to the extent of avoiding a situation. You therefore might miss great opportunities and keep your self-esteem to a low level. You don't have to be perfect, you need understand that you don't have to blame yourself for little imperfections because they don't have any impact on your worth or value as a person. In the long term, they really have no power over you.

So now the question is: how do I switch from self-criticism to self-confidence? Well, let's take one step at a time. The first stage is to accept yourself as you are. Self-acceptance might sound so tough and maybe even impossible but it is the key to unlocking your self-confidence and boosting your self-esteem.

Coming to peace with who you really are and your true self can be a pretty painful process, especially if you've been living almost all your life hating or distrusting yourself. It's time to stop. We need to actually see what beautiful human beings we are. We need to learn to embrace both our qualities and imperfections. We need to learn how to see ourselves from other's perspective.

One exercise that is always a great step in digging deeper into our self-image is to write down a list of our qualities. Think of all the good things you are able to do every day. Don't take anything for granted. This is the real secret. You can't take yourself for granted. Just like in a relationship or a marriage it's not healthy to take your partner for granted, you don't have to take yourself for granted either. You have to celebrate all the little wins and all the big wins. If you can park the car flawlessly, that is a great quality. "Oh but all drivers can park a car!" Nuh-uh! Some people are good at driving through little streets, some drivers master a night ride while others can't even move through the dark streets and others are good at parking the car. And why not give yourself some credit for it?

I haven't gone into details so far, but I will cover this now. Low self-esteem can come from your self-image in regards to any aspect of your life. It can be your body image that brings your confidence down. If you look in the mirror and start criticizing your physical aspect, then your self-esteem will be impacted and it will affect all areas of your life. Your lack of self-esteem, due to your body image, will prevent you from making friends, applying for your dream job or even falling in love. You will have this image in your head that everyone sees you as too thin, too fat, too tall, too short etc. and this will keep you from enjoying your life. You will see it in black and white and you won't be able to allow people to get close to you on an emotional level because you will be afraid they judge you behind your back.

Let me tell you the ugly truth! You won't like it but you will see how helpful it is! Nobody gives a damn about the body that you are so ashamed of. They all have better things to do when they go home than to judge you. And even if they do, how does that affect you? How does that devalue you? I know it sounds harsh at first, but give it a second thought, all of the above is just in your head. I warned you there was going to be some tough love in here. Point is, you'd better get happy with the body you have because you are living in it day in and day out.

To be honest, it kind of goes the same with any other flaw that you see in yourself as a deal-breaker. Whether it is your skills, what you are good at, your personality or your knowledge, you have to work through it yourself.

This part of the chapter is about you seeing your qualities beyond what you usually let yourself be convinced of. Write down anything that comes to mind and keep writing across a whole week. It takes a lot of self-observation depending on how low your self-esteem level is.

Now, actually making a change and improving your self-image won't come easy. The thing is, that the image we have about ourselves is projected on how others see us.

When we *disconsider* ourselves, this will impact the way we act, and we will end up sabotaging ourselves. Acting without confidence will prevent us from doing the best we can or being the best versions of ourselves. Therefore, the people around us will see the same.

Perhaps it is your closest friends that know the real you because they took the time to know you and see beyond your insecurities. Well, it's time to rely on their help now! Take a break from reading this book, put it aside for the next 10 minutes and send a text, a message or an email to at least three of your close friends. Ask them how they see you, what qualities they see in you. Tell them it is for a personal project that you are starting. You may or may not tell them this personal project is about you and your personal development, but pass the ball to them. You might even discover strengths you had no idea that you had. Then you can add them to your qualities list.

After you have done work on your self-acceptance, and you start being more comfortable in your own skin, it's time to move to the next level. It's time to start building your self-confidence. Easy to say, hard to do, you might think.

Yes, you are right to an extent. No one said overcoming low self-esteem or finding the path to happiness would be easy. What matters is that it is worth it.

So, in order to take the first steps towards your confidence, I challenge you to get out of your comfort zone. Get out of it in order to start learning new skills. Start doing things that you are passionate about and also good at. Being good at something gives you a boost in self-esteem straight away. Winning a competition or being rewarded for your success will make you jump out of your skin with joy. Staying stuck in a job or in a relationship that you don't like just because you are in your comfort zone and you don't take changes very well will keep your self-esteem at the same levels. However, making a change and getting out of your comfort zone will wake you up. Learning new things and doing something for your own benefit will increase that self-worth.

When I decided to end a relationship that wasn't making any of the parties involved happy, I started my blog. When I had another heartbreak, I launched a story-sharing platform. When I stopped dating, I decided to write a book. It's moments of change that shape us without even realising, because we end up putting our energy into something that is dear to our heart, things that perhaps we have been neglecting. We switch our focus. We channel all our pain into productivity. We end up rediscovering ourselves.

These moments that boost our productivity contribute to boosting our self-confidence too. That is why I am challenging you to make a change in your life right now! Get out of your comfort zone. We have already established that continuing in this way will not take you anywhere. So go out there, start a course, pick up a new hobby, learn new skills, get better at whatever you are already doing, just make a change. Make a list of your goals, just like you've learned in chapter 5, and start from there.

And since we are at it, let's also make a change in the people we hang out with. As I said, the image we have about ourselves is projected onto how others see us, but at the same time the image that other people might have about themselves might impact you without knowing it. So as part of your journey, give yourself the gift of hanging out with quality people.

Ok, I think I've already been giving you a lot of tough love and lessons, but I have to. And since you're so far along in this chapter, just bear with me a little longer because I am going to explain immediately what I mean by quality people.

I happen to believe all people have something good in them. I always try to see that positive side. Sometimes, as much as I try and even if I do see it, there are negatives that can throw a big shadow over the positive side. And yes, I used to hang out with some of them just because I knew deep down they were good persons and I was trying to hold on to that initial opinion. No matter how much they would eventually hurt me, I still ended up giving them a chance.

You see, though giving people a second chance comes from your best intentions and from a place of good, it doesn't always meet similar intentions on the other side. Sometimes, there is no point in continuing to keep these kinds of people in your life.

I truly believe that people have a certain energy that comes from within. It is exhaled through their very pores. So as soon as you meet and start talking to a stranger, you can get their positive or negative energy. It may be what others call a "first impression", but I like to think about it on a more energetic level.

Having moved twice outside my home country, I have developed the skill of making new friends quickly. This has only strengthened my belief in the human kind. I know we are attracted to people with the same energy level and I mean this in a purely interactive way, not sexually. Even after a long conversation with people, without coming from the same level of energy there was never a follow up. I have also met strangers and just connected in a matter of minutes. We instantly became friends or business buddies. It's not something palpable or that can be explained. It is pure intuition. But the people who bring your vibes up to the sky and who make you feel at the highest level of comfort and confidence are the ones you need to stick around.

There will be cases when you will find yourself surrounded by persons with low vibrations. Maybe even some of your existing acquaintances, friends or even closer people like your partner or members of your family. If we are talking about people that you can keep at a distance for a while, for all means do so until you are healed from low self-esteem. Once you meet their low vibrations with high energy, which is your aim once your self-confidence goes through the roof, you will be prepared. Until then, you need to be careful, since you are on your own journey of healing and personal development and you are vulnerable. Your first reaction will be to fix them, but don't. We all take our own journey and there is only so much we can do before it gets reflected on us.

When we have low self-esteem we attract people with the same level of self-esteem. They may seem strong and independent and confident on the surface, but their insecurities will come out in unexpected ways and they will have an impact on you. When making new friends, or just networking, you will see what kind of people are drawn to you. It goes the same in your dating life. A person with low self-esteem is tempted to chase an apparently confident individual, but they end up with someone who has a similar level of self-worth. And coming from a low vibe, they will try to bring you down as well. You always want to go up, so that is when you need to escape.

Let me tell you a short story. I once started dating a guy who seemed so grounded and sure of himself. At the time, I was coming from a previous relationship where I had dealt with uncertain grounds. I needed stability and certainty. I thought I had found it. There wasn't anything too romantic between us and we were both aware it wasn't going to lead anywhere long term, but we kept going out.

My level of self-esteem had already been shaken by the previous guy when I realised that I was accepting things I would normally consider repulsive. Like open relationships. Or being insulted. Somehow, I would always end up being the one apologising. I wasn't actually aware of how I got so entangled in that sort of rapport with this man, but his own insecurities coming from his own inner struggles affected me through time. Deep down, I wanted to help him, to rescue him because I could probably see the similarities between us.

I ended up with such low self-esteem that after we finally ended, I embarked on the most important healing journey of my life. It wasn't the first time I had hit rock bottom, therefore I had the advantage of already knowing what tools could help me. And Tinder was not one of them.

I knew that writing was going to save me, but it was the first time in my life when I just couldn't write. I would sit down in front of the laptop with the intention to type away a blog post but I felt so ashamed. I was embarrassed of telling the story of how I permitted myself to get in the position of being insulted by a man. And forgiving him. And allowing him to actually make me the guilty one. I took a three-month break from writing. Every attempt to put down the words meant digging down into my feelings. And there was no heart break or suffering, there was just shame. It took a lot of inner work. Then one Friday I just hopped on a train from London to Paris with a notebook and pen and spent a weekend writing it all out!

The reason I told you this story is to make you understand that we may not realise at first the reasons why we are attracted to certain type of individuals, either romantically or just socially. When we have low vibes, we will attract low vibes. Our subconscious will push us to rescue them when in fact we need to rescue ourselves first. Through interactions, others can impact our self-esteem in the way they talk or act, because it comes from a place of their own insecurities. Write down what kind of emotions are triggered inside of you after you talk to different people. At first you might miss the flags, but if you start writing you will see things from a clearer perspective. It will make you develop the skill of connecting to one's vibrational level and making a decision during the interaction itself. It takes practice though, so keep up the writing.

On the other hand, when we interact from a high vibrational state, we just attract like-minded persons and we can make friends for life. Luckily, I have plenty of these examples in my journey too.

Let's recap, where are we in our self-esteem journey? We've acknowledged it. We've discovered the symptoms and identified the negative self-beliefs. We've become aware of self-criticism. We accepted ourselves as we are and started boosting our self-confidence with activities that we are good at and that make us feel good. We've also gone through a little bit of an energetic declutter by putting on pause or removing for good the relationships with low-vibe individuals in our lives.

What next? Well, as I have just mentioned, keeping your self-esteem up requires you to hang out with quality people. You need to be supported. And who is the best quality person in your life that has always been there for you? It's yourself!

So it's time to learn the art of self-love. Make time for being just by yourself. Meditate. Listen to music. Sit on a bench in the park while people-watching. Do yoga. Go for a run. Grab your favourite coffee. Light a scented candle. Take a bath. Anything. Just make time for it!

My first tip is to schedule time in your agenda for self-care. And what's even more important, make it non-negotiable. That's right. If you have your Wednesday evening scheduled for some self-pampering and your workmates ask you to join them for happy hour, you will need to find the strength to say no. It doesn't matter what those plans are, because you are booked for the evening! You need to learn to make your self-care schedule a must in your agenda and just like any other planned meeting, you cannot allow yourself to postpone it. Write it down, plan for it and then write about it.

Secondly, build a self-care routine. Either it is a morning routine or an evening routine, either you choose to do it daily or weekly, just make sure to do it on a regular basis and not skip it. I personally have my morning routine diversified, but I never skip meditation. If there is a day when I don't meditate, I immediately feel the shakiness of my inner balance. I easily get annoyed, I can't focus and I even feel a physical discomfort in some cases. So I try to stick to my meditation routine in 90 percent of cases. Again, your routine can include literally anything that brings you joy and makes you feel spoiled and pampered. Remember, showing yourself love is the best way to lift your self-esteem and to connect with your inner self.

Lastly, self-love means being in tune to your true desires and your emotions. This leads to making decisions based on true feelings, without allowing the voice of fear and ego to take over and make that decision for you. It has to come from a place of pure awareness and mindfulness, which is something I am going to cover in more depth in the next chapter. Main thing is, we need to take ourselves into consideration when we make a decision.

One of the most powerful tools for self-love is affirmation. This relates to the little voice in your head that might still get out of control from time to time. Affirmations are the solution to reprogram your subconscious. They contribute greatly to positive thinking. When I started doing my affirmations, I didn't find the practice very reliable, so I had to include it in my meditation.

Many people have affirmations on their list for their morning routine and they just say whatever they get used to saying. It is on auto-pilot, they don't even believe it anymore. And then they wonder why it is not working. Well, you can't trick the Universe, you have to believe in what you are saying to yourself.

The exercise I found particularly useful for me is to write down a series of affirmations in relation to your goals. Put them on post-its and stick them around the house in the most visible places, where you will besure notto miss them. Stick them on your bathroom mirror, on your door, on the kitchen furniture or even on the coffee mug. You will have a double win from this exercise: the simple act of writing them down is engraving them in your subconscious, then seeing them all the time will trigger you to read them, or even say them out loud, and this will ground you in the present moment.

In conclusion to this chapter, I want to emphasize how important the work for your self-esteem is. If you don't lift your esteem, you can miss so many good chances in your life. But once the work is done, don't ever think that's it! I made this mistake. I was so sure I was in a good place after going through therapy and doing my inner work that I just went on with my life from a place of cockiness and feeling like I was untouchable. Guess what? There is such a fine line between walking on the cliff and falling in the abyss. And I fell.

Be careful. Keep in mind we are all a work in progress. Low self-esteem can kick back at any time, triggered by fear and acting as a defence mechanism that wants to bring us back to our comfort zone. We are all on a continuous journey and this is the beauty of it. We can keep falling, but we learn our lesson. It becomes a matter of how fast we come back.

So my dear, keep writing. Keep a journal for self-observation. Always refer back to it when you feel in danger of slipping away from your core of confidence.

Be in a permanent search, stay grateful, treat yourself with care, give yourself recognition for the small and big accomplishments. Write down what gets triggered by your mind subconsciously and see which areas need focus. Never neglect your self-esteem. Don't confuse caring for yourself with being full of yourself, which is just being arrogant on the surface. Being self-confident can manifest in many ways without needing the attention and validation of anyone around you.

CHAPTER 8

Writing for mindfulness

If we look at the dictionary's definition of writing, there are multiple ways to describe the activity itself. Most of the definitions refer to a means of communication, of translating signs or symbols on a surface or a means of expression. My personal favourite one is "writing is making a permanent impression of something".

Making an impression is usually regarded as a shallow way of living. It's frequently stated that you don't have to impress anyone. And I couldn't agree more. You don't have to impress anyone. But you should impress yourself. You should be your biggest fan and celebrate all your small accomplishments, just like we've discussed in the previous chapter.

The other aspect of making an impression comes also from a question we often ask ourselves: "How do I want to be remembered?" What impression do you want to leave to your kids, your grandkids, your friends and all the people you come across during your life? Nobody wants to be invisible. Especially if it comes from a place of helping and being kind to others in a sense that you leave a mark on other people's lives.

We want to make a difference in this world. We want to leave our footprints for humanity and we want to lead by example. We want to help other people. And there are so many people who do it already. It is not about taking pride in it or expecting anything in return, but being the hero of our families, of other people's lives and of our communities, which make our hearts glow. And it can only come from a place of pure kindness, of gratitude and peace with ourselves first. It means making an impression and being remembered.

At the same time, making an impression is also about having your own impressions about the outside world. It means making your own opinions, without allowing other people to influence you. It means strongly believing in what makes sense for you. It means having your impressions about the aspects of life that matter for you and shape who you are. It means creating opinions and memories that last.

And what better way of keeping a record of your memories than writing them down? Making your impressions last longer is a way of being in tune with your inner self, of being aware of what makes your heart happy and joyful.

Let's take for example a trip that you go on. You travel, take photos, make memories. If you travel with a group of friends, you will all have memories of that trip. Years later, you will realise that each of you has kept a slightly different impression of the trip. You can rely on your friends' impressions, or you can keep a recording of your own impressions. What would you choose?

The most important thing is that in order to be able to take in impressions and opinions without being judgemental, you need to be mindful. You need to be present and aware of what goes on around you. You need to be centred with your inner self and pay attention. As we have covered in one of the previous chapters, writing is one of the activities that keeps you grounded, focused and connects your inner self with the outside world.

When we choose to let ourselves be impressed by the outside world, we have millions of thoughts going through our minds. Sometimes, these thoughts are not even comprehensible, because we just don't pay attention to them. We pick one thought, go with it, carry it through either a past memory or a future scenario and we go until our train of thought is interrupted.

As soon as we start paying attention and listening to these thoughts as a witness, looking at them with objectivity or perhaps like watching a movie at the cinema, we start making sense of what is happening. Then follows the simple action of connecting our brain with our hands and translating those signals into words that we write down on paper. And so our impressions are now recorded.

If you truly want to make a lasting impression and allow a certain situation to be impregnated in your memory, then you'd better write it down. When you write it, you are there. You bring back into your mind's eye the memory, or you imagine a scene from the future. Either way, you visualise it in your mind while writing it down and you are there. You are focused.

You may be a fan of multitasking – I am too – but if you think about something else while writing your impressions, it won't work. If other thoughts interrupt your flow, you will stop writing. Just test it. Try to sing a song in your head all while writing down about how you spent your previous weekend. I challenge you. And even if you do it, I bet you won't be pleased with the result. When you write you need to focus. You need to go into that zone of recreating that scene, feeling those feelings and actually paying attention to the words you put down so that your writing makes sense.

As a mindful activity, writing offers structure to our thoughts. Instead of getting lost in them, we put them in order. The genuine therapeutic benefit of writing is when you actually listen to your mind. You allow yourself to pay attention to whatever comes to mind. You don't ignore it, instead you stay with it, listen to it like you would listen to the stories of a good friend, and then you let your hand take action.

Handwriting has this therapeutic effect. Writing with pen on paper makes you even more sensitive to your thoughts for several reasons. First of all, because handwriting is slower than typing, it makes your thoughts slow down too. Instead of rushing through your thoughts, they stay at a reasonable speed. They take longer in unfolding because there is a story that is being created in your mind. Secondly, handwriting gives you contact with the paper, with the pen or pencil. It keeps you in the here and now. You can focus on forming the letters, on typography, on being quicker or slower.

In the book *Writing Down the Bones - Freeing the Writer Within*, Natalie Goldberg explains the act of handwriting in the most beautiful way, "handwriting is more connected to the movement of the heart. The inside world creates the outside world, but the outside world and our tools also affect the way we form our thoughts."

Perhaps you can let your mind wander when the act of writing itself becomes automatic. This is like in the cases when you just perform an action of copying a transcript without paying any attention to the words you lay on paper. No. When we truly write from the heart and with our minds, then it is an absolute requirement to stay with the thoughts and follow them down the line.

In fact, if you truly stay within yourself and keep writing, you might experience a state of flow. If you don't know what I'm talking about, this is a concept that professor Mihaly Csikszentmihalyi wrote books about and conducted research on. Let me give you an example. Think of an activity you like to do. Perhaps playing a sport, running, dancing, cooking, cleaning the house, playing a video game or repairing your car. You just lose track of time. There is no early or late. Time seems to have stopped. There is no sense of "I can't wait to get this over with." Instead you just indulge yourself into it to an extent that you no longer pay attention to your watch. You are no longer tired or hungry, you don't feel the need to get up or step out. You are not bored, you are challenged. You just let yourself go with the flow and at the end, when you get out of the zone, you just feel like time flew by. Five hours feel like five minutes. You feel as if you have woken from a dream.

It is the best feeling in the world when you do something you are passionate about. When you enter that state of flow, your level of happiness goes through the roof! You just forget about anything else and you go into the zone. Any sort of activity that is done in a state of flow brings your happiness to its peaks.

You've probably heard many artists (or maybe you are one of them) who say they go into the zone when they create. Painting, drawing, sculpting, composing, writing music or editing a movie can be examples of activities that bring creators in a state of flow. Think about sportsmen. Tennis players for instance need to be in a state of flow when they play in competitions. If their mind starts wandering, they lose focus and they allow their thoughts to invade their inner space and they miss points. They make mistakes. They lose.

When writing, it is about entering that state of flow. It is about making the action of writing something that you just can't stop doing because it brings you to such a level of being present and mindful that you just don't want to stop it.

Of course, flow is not the only way to be happy when writing. You can find many ways to use writing for your happiness. After all, it is all about indulging in the activity, it is about finding activities that lift your spirit in every way possible. Keep looking for those hobbies that keep you passionate about life and keep you mindful. It is about sky-rocketing your happiness.

Since we are touching base with the concept of happiness, and this is a very dear subject to my heart, I will take the opportunity to expand a little bit on the topic. You see, I've been in search of happiness for a while. I questioned what happiness was. I wanted to live it, to feel it, but I didn't know what to expect, how it is supposed to feel. One of the books that became a guide for me in my journey was *The How To Happiness* by Sonya Lyubomirski. It had been recommended to me by my therapist when I used to go to sessions. It just happened that I spotted it in a bookstore when I needed it most. I guess the Universe works in miraculous ways after all.

One of the concepts that truly stayed with me was about the baseline of happiness. We are all born with a baseline of happiness, which is basically our genetic predisposition towards happiness, that comes from our ancestors, in a combination of genes. There are both good parts and bad parts about it if you think about it.

If you are lucky to be born with a high baseline of happiness, then you can definitely see the good parts. You are already from birth happier than the average population and this translates in seeing the world around you in a more positive way, being more optimistic and maybe more forgiving. Now this baseline counts for 50 percent of your overall happiness. Meaning that if you are not lucky enough and you come from a background with less happy genes, you still have plenty of space to improve that.

I like to think that happiness is a state of mind, that we can reprogram our minds to be happier and we can influence our level of joy consciously. I've tried it and it works. When I have mornings that I cannot get out of bed, I just start smiling. Even if I feel tired or upset, which of course is for apparently no reason, I just say something nice to myself and I smile. I smile like I mean it. And my brain believes it. And I wake up happier. And it works throughout the day as well. Of course, it takes more effort and determination to uplift a level that by default comes as a low one, but it is worth it. It can only be done if the person is aware of this possibility.

Writing is one way of finding your flow to boost your happiness level. Believe it or not, it doesn't even matter what you write about. Let's try the following exercise, known as a channelling exercise.

Be in a comfortable position, in a safe environment, where you can relax. This works in moments you want to calm yourself. Take a few long deep breaths, then channel your inner voice onto paper. Write about anything. Write about whatever it is that crosses your mind. This is your Higher Self sending you a message. Write about good or bad. Write about feelings, even though it may look like they make no sense at first or that they just seem to come from nowhere. When you begin writing them down it will start to make sense.

Write continuously for five minutes. Maybe even set up your alarm clock. Or don't. You might be surprised to see that once you are in a state of flow, you won't even realise how fast time goes. Don't lift your pen from the paper, just continue writing. Channel your inner voice and let everything come out. Even the embarrassing thoughts or the ones you wish you wouldn't have. Accept them and write them down.

Another way to connect with your thoughts and feelings before you start writing them down is by practicing meditation. This will help you tremendously if you notice you are having trouble getting into that inner state of being with your thoughts. Try silent meditations and connect with yourself. Try guided meditation. It will help you reveal emotions that you didn't even know you were hiding in there.

Perhaps create a visualisation in your mind that will help trigger the flow of thoughts and emotions that have been hiding away for so long. Set an intention for the long or short term and see it with your mind's eye. I've had some purely golden revelations during meditation. Some of the things that came up to the surface surprised me to such an extent that I came out of the meditation crying. The important thing is to listen during that meditation. Then you can write whatever comes to the surface. This will liberate you. Meditation brings you the ultimate state of mindfulness. Writing after it is just the way of letting it all out from your mind onto the paper as a release.

Another way of including writing as a mindful activity in your daily routine is to write your dreams after you wake up. I know. You may tell me you don't believe in dreams and in their meaning, and maybe I don't always try to see meaning in them either, but dreams seem to be the way that the unconscious communicates to us.

Keep a notebook or a journal next to your bed, so that you can write it down as soon as you wake up. You might want to look up the meaning of your dream and try to find out what your subconscious is trying to tell you. Besides, you know when you have one of those dreams that just makes you wake up with a wide smile on your face? And then five minutes later you just completely forget what it was about? Don't let it slip away. Write it down as soon as you wake up and it can even be a fun way of remembering what you have dreamt about.

No matter what kind of activity you perform at any given time, be it writing or something else, you need to make sure you are mindfully engaging in it. Even walking can be done mindfully. You might try a walking meditation. It will still make you engaged and immersed, even in the simple action of stepping. Pay attention to the contact of your feet with the ground with every step you take. Pay attention to the shift of your weight from one leg to the other. Look around, breathe in the smells, look at the colours, listen to the sounds. Be mindful, be present in your walk. We tend to just rush every day. We end up rushing through life. We forget to simply pay attention to the simple things around us.

We can simply transform any activity that is part of our routine into a pleasurable one if we put mindfulness into it. Washing the dishes or taking a shower can be seen as more than just things we need to do every day. We can think about them as being our refuge from the rush of life. It's a true blessing to find a way to perform daily activities with mindfulness.

Besides, if you also end up writing about them, it will make you even more mindful, by the simple act of connecting through the moments of focus and looking within.

I know I've already mentioned multitasking earlier in this chapter, but I want to point something out in relation to mindfulness. In the corporate world, and most of the time, even at home, we are expected to multitask. Like gracefully stir the pan while speaking on the phone and cleaning the sink with the other hand. Or replying to emails, chatting with your colleagues and eating. Well, no! When you do multiple things at a time, your brain can only concentrate on one of them. So the rest are performed on auto-pilot mode. There is no presence and mindfulness in that.

Multitasking is a misconception of productivity. In fact, we are not productive at all, because we end up doing halves of each activity instead of dedicating ourselves 100 percent to one thing at a time and doing it the best we can.

Plus, multitasking kills creativity. If you want to be able to express yourself in a creative way and connect with your inner personality, multitasking is not the answer. In order to get in the zone and fall under that incredible flow that lifts up your happiness level, you need to be focused, present, grounded, not distracted. You can only observe feelings and sensations when you are actually engaged in that one single activity.

When it comes to writing, you might find it useful to have some music in the background. That is perfectly fine, as long as it doesn't become a distraction, as long as you don't get your attention stolen away by the lyrics or a disturbing tune. Keep it at a low volume, perhaps just an instrumental choice. Focus instead on your thoughts when you do writing exercises.

As I've just mentioned, you might need to get into that creative mood before your emotions are triggered and before you get your thoughts flowing. Just make sure you know what makes your creative juices flow and use that for expressing yourself. After all, any creative activity is an expression of the artist's inner struggles, an expression from unspoken words.

While you get into that flow, you won't even notice that your senses become more in tune to the action you are doing. For instance, when writing, your eyes will stay focused on the piece of paper, your ears will start hearing the sound of the pen running on the piece of paper, or you might hear the cadence of the keyboards when you type at your computer. You might even start seeing the letters forming or become aware of your hand movements. You might smell the ink or the paper. All your senses become engaged in the activity of writing. You are mindfully engaged. There is no room for multitasking.

Mindfulness brings out hidden feelings if we learn how to listen and pay attention to our inner voice and sensations. It reveals unknown corners where beliefs that you are not very proud of hide. All we need to do is allow it. We need to listen and our mind will become a land to explore. By writing down our thoughts and feelings and going through the process of self-discovery, we see how we have changed through time, how we have grown and how experience influences our judgments and perceptions. We grow up. The way we see things changes. We see the same thing through different filters every single time. But only when we mindfully make that connection with ourselves will we be able to reveal all of it!

CHAPTER 9

Writing Therapy kit

One of my favourite things about using writing techniques for healing and improving our quality of life is its accessibility. If you think about it as a form of therapy, in comparison to speaking to a therapist, writing is more personal. It can be the first step that one can take in order to face their fears before expressing them to a stranger.

Some people consider going to therapy to be shameful and it's something I've addressed here in the first chapter. There are various misconceptions about what therapy is, how it works and what are the expectations. On the same level, as a coach myself, I encounter many people confusing therapy and coaching and that is an honest mistake. These topics are so undermined by the society that people feel embarrassed to seek for help. And when they do, they realise there are so many options out there for them, they just weren't aware of them.

I'm not going to go deeper into the matter of counselling, therapy or coaching, but it's important to say that they are both helpful when you find yourself stuck.

Don't be ashamed to ask for help and support, there will always be someone out there who can give you a hand. Besides, every coach has a different approach. That is the beauty in finding a good fit and connection.

When it comes to writing as a tool for therapeutic benefits, I found it to be easy and effective. It simply makes such a big difference to whatever you are going through. No matter where you go from there, you will find it useful to keep writing as part of your life.

Therapy sessions are traditionally seen as meetings with a specialised therapist to discuss the patient's problems. With the rise of the alternative therapies, people have found that they can take action for themselves and go for self-help if they don't want to reach out to a therapist. Instead they have all sorts of tools that help them connect with themselves and perhaps forget about their issues.

Although they might seem like distractions, people who practice alternative therapies find a refuge from the monkey-mind in these activities. It is a way to become present, engaged, to surrender to the moment and quiet one's thought.

In short, alternative therapy is anything that is not traditional therapy, just like alternative medicine is anything that is not considered standard medical care. Alternative therapy is quite often an artistic activity, given that artists are known to go into flow when they create, releasing stress and increasing happiness levels.

Anything from drawing, to painting, sculpting, dancing, playing an instrument, singing, gardening, any creative act or do-it-yourself can be seen as an alternative therapy if performed regularly for improving the stress levels. Writing is one of them. If we want to be pragmatic, it is probably the cheapest too. I mean, you just need a pencil and basically anything can become your paper - back of a book, napkin, supermarket receipt and so on.

Besides, you don't have to be a writer in order to use writing for healing purposes. Everyone can write if you know how to write. Assuming you are reading this book, or can afford to even think about self-care and self-help, you have gone through school. You are familiar with the act of writing and reading.

The funny thing is, we already use writing in our day to day lives so often that we use it in ways we don't even realise. If you write a grocery shopping list, it is writing. You order your thoughts, you put them down so that you have a structure when you visit the supermarket. You can go one step further and structure the list to the extent of the order of the aisles in the shop. Whatever floats your boat.

Or when you write an email, it reflects your inner voice. No matter how business-related it is, you still put the words down, words filtered through your mood that day. With every piece of writing we leave a piece of us behind.

Now as I've already mentioned, writing is cheaper than any other alternative art. If you think about it, a pen will be less expensive than a brush and colours, or a guitar. Nobody says you can't go crazy with writing too. I personally go crazy around stationery. I'm a big fan of handwriting. Most of the time, I've noticed that it helps to have a writing instrument above the average pencil and the A4 blank piece of paper. Especially for the people who are trying to find any excuse to stay away from writing, stationery can be the answer.

Remember how in school we would buy colourful pencil cases and all those stickers for our notebooks? They were all meant to make us more passionate about studying and doing our homework. This is because we will always be more tempted to react to aesthetics and beauty as human beings.

In terms of writing instruments, you have so many options that I feel no matter how long my list will be, I'm still not going to cover all of them. In an attempt to give you an idea, please do feel free to choose any of the following: pencil, pen, fountain pen, colourful pens, markers, coloured pencils, ink-based pens, gel-based pens and so on. It is after all your choice that represents you best. A choice that excites you to grab that pen and write.

You have just as many options for paper too! Colour, smell, texture, the choices are limitless. If you are a very organised type of person, you might want to go with linear paging, or perhaps some other guiding boxes and lines instead of blank pages.

The cheapest is the classical A4 sheet. Or better yet, cheaper than cheapest is to just write out your feelings on a used newspaper, or the back of a used book or napkins. Just find something to write on. There is just something special about seeing those letters form by hand on paper. Paper is always there for you, just waiting for you to fill it with words. Paper will never tell. It never rushes. Paper is your confident.

Of course, if you are serious about writing and using it long term, which I obviously strongly advise you to be, then you might want to invest in a notebook or a diary. Again, all stationery shops have so much to offer when it comes to notebooks that it is sometimes painful to think that you can only write with one hand and that you can only fill so many pages in a lifetime. Go with whichever suits your preferences.

Quality is one of the factors to take into consideration. I refer here to both the quality of the pages as well as the quality of the cover. You might prefer leather covers or sparkling colours on a hard cover.

The next level is to get a customized notebook, with bespoke lettering and messages on the cover. Even the inside pages' design is entirely up to you. Size-wise, you can have a mini-notebook to carry around with you where you can put down ideas that come to your mind - as a replacement of the memos on your smartphone. I advise that you have an A5 diary or notebook for home use as well, because it might feel more comfortable to confess deeper thoughts while in a safe space rather than scribbling away on the tube.

A trend that has begun to increase lately is bullet journaling. This is for the persons who prefer structure, organisation, layout. It structures the way you journal by giving you prompts and pre-defined pages for you to fill in. It helps with inspiration if you feel stuck when staring at a blank sheet of paper. However, it goes against the free flow of writing and I like to encourage people to think and write outside the box. If you are one of those who wouldn't go over the lines in the colouring books when you were a kid, then this might feel frustrating if you find yourself in the position of wanting to express more than the space provided. On the other hand, it is a great way to start journaling if you are reluctant to the idea.

So just to summarize this first part of the chapter regarding the writing kit, whenever you put pen to paper, it connects us better with our thoughts. Your wiring from your brain to your hand is in fact the translation of your emotions into words and onto paper. Even though you are translating the language of the mind in the most common words you are achieving something beyond ordinary. The whole process of writing will not allow your thoughts to rush, they will flow and become structured, they will start making sense.

If you are not a fan of writing by hand or you just want to give other options a try, or you are writing a manuscript, I got you covered.

Who wouldn't love an old-fashioned typewriter? I am crazy about these pure pieces of art, especially the vintage models. Most of all because they hold a story, they have been touched by the fingers of writers who used them to put words onto paper to tell a story and share it with the world. You can just imagine what hidden secrets the typewriter keeps. They're treasures.

Of course, I wanted to go with the bohemian and romantic option first - the typewriter- just to delay the obvious. Computers and laptops give us access to a whole new level of writing. Typing is preferable when you write volumes, for instance I am typing the content of this book on my laptop - following my handwritten outline. When it comes to typing long texts on the other hand, you might find that typing on a computer manages to keep up with your process of thought. However, it can tend to feel impersonal and cold, so it is less advisable to type away your feelings and emotions like this. Unless you want to share your story on your blog, send them by email or write them in a manuscript, I would suggest sticking with pen and paper.

Nevertheless, there is always the on-the-go option, the tool you keep in your pocket or in your bag every day. Your smartphone. I personally struggle with typing on my smartphone even if it is just a text message. If I get frustrated by the autocorrect or my fingers hitting the wrong letters and buttons, my emotions are suddenly about that and I can't really follow my train of thought. It can be a great choice for typing something you don't want to forget about, make a note, or just send yourself an email to remind you of it. This is why the mini-notebook would be the best idea, but if you don't keep it with you, then the smartphone will certainly do. So type away!

Covering the tools part - both analogue and digital - leads us to discovering other aspects of what constitutes a writing kit. Let's talk about the environment.

You want to sit in a comfortable position, but maybe not too relaxed, as you need to keep your muscles engaged so your whole body will perceive your activity. It makes such a difference. Ideally when writing or typing you want to sit upright on a chair, at a table, with both your feet on the ground and your elbows on the table at a 90-degree angle. Sounds technical, right? It is a postural piece of advice, but you will understand after you try it.

You can of course sit cross-legged or lay down in a bed or a hammock. However, the most comfortable position will always be the one that your body associates with this activity.

When it comes to the environment, we will just presume that you have a choice. You can write at home or in a cafe. I personally find myself very inspired in cafes because it involves watching people. Instead of being distracted by them it actually wakes up new ideas in my head and perhaps triggers new emotions to explore.

For example, I was once in front of a cafe at a table typing away, and there were many children walking by from the school across the street. I found myself really emotional, so I decided to explore the feeling. I closed the Word document I was writing in and opened a new one and started typing on a blank sheet of paper all the triggered thoughts and emotions. And oh boy, the things that came out of that impromptu session were incredible!

When you write from your safe place at home, you might prefer it to be quiet or you might play a little bit of music in the background. You might want to sit by the window or you might choose to write after dark, next to a candle. Find your cosy spot and just use it for journaling or for free writing sessions, channelling your thoughts onto paper.

My favourite part is the accessories that we can choose to use if we want to create a ritual for writing. Here I am referring to having a scented candle or scented sticks nearby. Or having your favourite mug filled with tea or coffee. Or wrapping yourself with the fluffiest blanket in your house to make yourself feel cosy and protected.

This is actually very well connected with the feeling of *hygge*, which is a Danish concept of happiness. There is no translation for it, but, if it comes from the nation that scored the title for the happiest place to live on Earth many years in a row, then we want to at least give it a try.

In *The Little Book of Hygge*, Meik Wiking, who is a researcher at the Happiness Institute in Copenhagen, writes: "Keep a nice notebook in your hygge emergency kit. We may call this your hygge journal. The first exercise is to note down some of the most hyggelige moments you have experienced in the past month or year. This will allow you to enjoy them again and make you mindful of which experiences you enjoyed. For the second exercise, think of what kind of hyggelige experiences you would like to have in the future. A bucket list of hygge, if you will."

After writing, either during your hygge experience or as part of your channelling, journaling or ad-hoc writing, you can again make your choice. You can keep the papers or save the documents in your computer and review them down the line to see the changes, to evaluate how the situation developed.

If it is too painful and you prefer instead to just adhere to the process of letting go, then you can tear apart or burn the pieces of paper you have written on. Or just delete them from your laptop. Don't forget to empty your recycle bin too! In dealing with pain and healing, you might seek purification and decluttering, to which I suggest getting rid of any piece of writing that contains your pain, your anger, your sadness. Let it go. You don't have to hold onto the past. This decision is just another part of your writing kit.

CHAPTER 10

Writing as a habit for happiness

I will be assuming that if you've got so far in this book, you are already starting to become a bit more familiar with writing and have maybe even given it a try. No pressure!

You've seen so far what an incredibly important role writing plays in healing and getting over some of the biggest emotional traumas. We've explored how writing can lift you up when you fall down and you desperately need to rise from the ashes. We've gone through types of writing, exercises and even tools.

Now, since you've become acquainted with the magic powers of writing - or maybe you knew it all along - I'd like for you to become friends with writing. Make writing your soul mate. Know that writing is there for you no matter what happens, for better or for worse. Writing is your key to happiness.

What happens most of the time is that people tend to be suspicious. Whenever I speak about writing, only those who have already given it a try know its powers, whereas the newbies are always a bit funny about the idea. *How could writing this letter help me? I have bigger problems. They won't get solved by writing about them...*

If only I had a penny for every time I heard that...

People will resist trying new things because we are used to having proved results. Most of the time it is difficult. It is choking and it can feel overwhelming to start writing. Humans are programmed to reject ideas that don't align with their belief system, their already established patterns.

If only they took a step back and put their beliefs aside, they could discover a whole new world out there. You have to be open-minded in order to embrace the magical things that can happen. Happiness has strange ways to creep up. We are scared about it because we think happiness is a goal, a destination. Wrong! Happiness is the road. Every day there is happiness. Every day there is joy and ease around us if we just stop to see it.

So instead of being afraid to embrace new practices that will uplift our happiness levels, why not give it a try? After all, suspicion can only be broken with trial. And if it doesn't work for you, then it's fine, your happiness might be in painting, or photography or singing. But how would you know if you haven't even given it a shot?

Think about when you first hopped on the driver's seat and touched the wheel, did you know what to do and how to drive the car? Or did you have to take lessons and be perseverant? It's the same with learning to play a musical instrument. You will have no clue how to handle a violin when you attempt to play it for the first time. Why would you assume that writing will be easy and that you will rock it from the first try?

Just like any other activity that you do in your life, when you don't put your heart into it honestly, it won't work. Then you'll swear at me and my book and my tips about writing. The truth is I can't control the amount of emotion you are willing to put into writing and how much you are willing to open up, especially if this is something that you are not comfortable with. Results will happen over time. The transformation can be magical if you're willing and open to trust the process. I mean, give the Universe some credit for allowing you to let go of the thoughts that you let go onto paper.

I get asked about when is the best time to write. I wish I could give you a secret recipe for this. In fact it is entirely up to you. Only you can try out different possibilities. Some people like writing first thing in the morning, before they even get out of bed, maybe because they have dreamt about something inspiring. Others dive into gratitude journaling right after their morning meditation. There are people who keep a small notebook with them and make notes, or pros and cons lists, throughout the day. Some choose to write before they go to bed so that they can release any emotions they have accumulated over the day before sleeping.

My advice in this sense would be to try out different times of the day. Try to avoid transforming writing into a burden, because you will easily switch it to auto-pilot mode and get disconnected when doing it. We don't want that to happen. This is not just an activity that needs to be checked off your to-do list, you need to really be mindful. Don't allow it to become boring. If you don't feel like writing, don't write. Allow it to come from within as a desire to release emotions and feelings.

It is said that it takes 21 days for a new habit to be formed, so try it out. Write for two, three, five minutes every day for 21 days. See what happens. Notice what changes. In some cases, you might find yourself running to your notebook and pen to write down your 'thank-you's if you are feeling gratitude for something that has happened to you. Or you might want to pour your anger into writing because you realise that it is much healthier to do so than to punch walls - or God forbid, other people.

Test your relationship with writing before making a decision or giving it up for good. Look at it as a way to climb the ladder of happiness instead of associating it continuously with negative stories. Try it, for better or worse.

Even when you really get into writing, you might experience points in your life when you feel like taking a break. And that is absolutely alright, especially when writing is part of your healing journey. As mentioned in the chapter about getting over trauma, writing comes into play only after the grief stage has ended. It's never healthy to skip this stage, as the grief will come back eventually stronger and more overwhelming.

I once watched a TED Talk by the novelist Ann Hood where she asks the question "Why Write." She beautifully explained how writing helps us make sense of the outside world. She also gave a very touching personal story about the loss of her daughter: "Grief and shock stopped the part of my brain that used language." It took her two years before she could start writing again.

So even when you get into the habit of writing and you find it to be the best expressive tool in the world, there are events that can happen in your life that can cut off that urge to put it all on paper. It is too painful. It is too difficult to make sense of the reality.

Once, after ending a toxic relationship, I felt too embarrassed to write. I had to deal with it first. I had to accept the outer reality before making sense of it. Once I allowed the pain to unravel, step by step, I wasn't afraid of a blank page anymore. I knew it was the lesson that had brought me down and I had the responsibility to pass it on to the world. And I started writing again. And all these experiences put me on the path of supporting other women going through tough times, breakups and toxic relationships. I've been there. I went through it. I found healing in writing, so you can too!

One way I suggest you to start writing, if you are more on the "this is not for me" side, is by putting down three things you are grateful for. It's the first step to stop seeing the world in a negative way and start getting an idea of all the positive things that you are taking for granted. Just start by noticing small things, like being thankful for the omelette that was really tasty this morning. Or go for bigger things, like thanking the Universe for making the sun come out on this beautiful day. It's up to you how you choose to start feeding that gratitude.

You might find it easier to make a gratitude list once a week rather than doing it every day when you are not used to it. What am I going to write in it every day? Well, once you understand the purpose of this exercise, you will begin to notice all the small things that you could be grateful for. Until then you can start practicing weekly so that you get a bigger picture of the positivity that awaits to be discovered.

It comes in handy especially when you go through trouble or stress. Instead of focusing on the bad vibes, switch your thoughts to focusing on the good surrounding you. It's important to make it part of your life, to pay attention to the things you already have instead of the things that you don't. The signals you send in the Universe when you think of all that you lack, are signals of ungratefulness for what you already have in your life, so the Universe will push back and say "Why would I give more to this person who doesn't appreciate what they already have? It means that even if I give them more, they will still want more and not appreciate it." It is the Law of Attraction. If you are not familiar with this law, please do allow yourself to find out more about it, as I am not going to dive deeper into it, but I will place some resources at the back of the book for those wanting to learn more.

In order to make writing a part of your daily activities, you can carry with you that small notebook I was telling you about in earlier chapters. Or you can just install an app on your smartphone where you can type away at any point during the day. A friend of mine gifted me one of these small notebooks and her instructions were: "Write something happy in it every day and then read it when you feel sad." I absolutely adore this idea and I encourage you to try it.

Feel free to put down a song you like, a joke you hear, the street name where that shop is located and so on. It's a great way to keep your memories in one place. You might want to go home and write in more detail about some of the things you sketch or maybe it can contribute to a larger set of ideas for one of your projects. Inspiration is all around us.

If you do get home and want to expand on your notes by writing or typing, make it personal, express emotions, use it as a journaling exercise. You might actually find that keeping a journal suits you better. The secret with it is to be honest and open, to put down more than just facts, to go deeper and explore the feelings that you've experienced during the day. Smells, tastes, anything that has stayed with you. As author Natalie Goldberg puts it, "This is naked writing. It is an opportunity to view ourselves and reveal ourselves as we truly are and to simply accept ourselves without manipulation and aggression. 'I am unhappy'- don't try to cover that statement up. Accept it without judgement if that's how you felt."

As told earlier in this book, I used to have a journal when I was younger. I was so terrified that anyone would read it. Even to the present day I keep writing my personal experiences, but now I'm not hiding it anymore. In fact I blog about it. My blog has become my journal. I write experiences from my dating life, from my travels, from my friends and family, from my work and so on. Hell, I am writing my first book here.

Another way to include writing in your day to day life - and you might be already doing it but don't really think too much of it - is by writing lists of pros and cons before making a decision. Write alternative options. Analyse the possible outcomes. Then, once you decide to go in one direction, keep track of it.

Write the advantages of walking down that route, write the lessons, write the pieces of advice you would give to someone in your own shoes. Never regret it. You have made the decision and you went all in. You can't change it so why torture yourself with regret? Find a solution instead and if you need to make a new decision, pull out a piece of paper and start making a new list of pros and cons.

Another practice I recommend for daily writing is based on affirmations. The power of affirmations stays in the way you tell them to yourself, whether it is in the mirror or during meditation or just in writing. It is all about being honest and trusting every single word. When writing down affirmations, feel free to customise your own affirmations or just write the ones that you have heard or read somewhere else. You can also write them on post-it notes and stick them around the house so that you can spot them several times during your day. And then repeat them to yourself. Because you will assimilate them once by writing and secondly by repeating them out loud.

Hopefully these ideas will have appealed to you and you will give writing a try. The power of writing is so great for healing and for happiness.

There are ways to connect with fellow writers in your communities if you want to start a writing group or run workshops. When I work with groups, people have some breakthrough transformations in just a couple of hours, so imagine what constant writing can do. Besides, bringing together people who love writing can be motivating and inspiring. It also fuels the feeling of belonging to a community. In time it builds trust. You may not feel comfortable to share your writing pieces with others at first, but once you start building that level of trust and confidence, you will begin opening up.

Another opportunity to hang out with people who are willing to use writing for making shifts in their life is by going to retreats. These can be either intensive weekends dedicated to expressive writing or they can be longer periods of time - one week, two weeks, one month. They can be combined with practices of meditation, and yoga perhaps, to enrich your spiritual healing and to get to a level of relaxation that will trigger the emotional writing.

Sometimes a simple change of scenery can be a sufficient trigger for emotional release. People are in some cases trapped in their daily routine, going to the same places, doing the same things, never actually taking the opportunity to feel their feelings. By stepping outside their familiar space, they instantly feel what has been missing, they understand how disconnected they have been and they start working towards reconnecting, rediscovering and healing.

Challenging as it may sound, the power of change stays in stepping outside the comfort zone. Once you give it a try you will know if writing is for you or not. Don't reject it just because of misconceptions and judgements.

Be open to explore it. Get your writing kit sorted out and start writing.

The good news about it is - and I'm sure you've already got this, but just to make sure, I'll repeat it - is that anyone can. You don't need to be a famous writer or artist, you don't need to feel the pressure to be creative. All you need to do is to listen to what is inside of you and write it. It works miracles!

Exercises sheet

Exercise Chapter 1

Write continuously for 1 minute about ANYTHING.

....
....
....
....
....
....
....
....
....
....
....
....
....
....
....
....
....
....
....
....
....
....
....
....
....

Exercise Chapter 2

Write about a situation that causes you stress.

....

....

....

....

....

....

....

....

....

....

....

....

....

....

....

....

....

....

....

....

....

....

....

....

....

Exercise Chapter 2

The STaF Exercise: Divide a piece of paper into three columns. The first column will be the Situation, the second column will be the Thoughts and the third column will be the Feelings.

SITUATION	THOUGHTS	FEELINGS

Exercise Chapter 5

If you imagine yourself in five years' time, how do you see yourself?

....
....
....
....
....
....
....
....
....
....
....
....
....
....
....
....
....
....
....
....
....
....
....
....
....
....
....
....

Exercise Chapter 5

Make a list of the things you know you have to do in the next month. Break it down and put deadlines next to each action that you need to take.

....
....
....
....
....
....
....
....
....
....
....
....
....
....
....
....
....
....
....
....
....
....
....
....
....
....
....
....
....

Exercise Chapter 6

Write a letter to someone who has acted in a wrongful way to you

....
....
....
....
....
....
....
....
....
....
....
....
....
....
....
....
....
....
....
....
....
....
....
....
....
....

Exercise Chapter 6

Write about your first kiss.

....
....
....
....
....
....
....
....
....
....
....
....
....
....
....
....
....
....
....
....
....
....
....
....
....
....
....
....
....
....

Exercise Chapter 7

Why do you think you are not good enough? What makes you think this? What happened in the past that made you think this about yourself?

....
....
....
....
....
....
....
....
....
....
....
....
....
....
....
....
....
....
....
....
....
....
....
....
....
....
....
....

Continue with "Who am I?", "What am I?", "Where am I meant to be?", "What am I meant to be?"

....
....
....
....
....
....
....
....
....
....
....
....
....
....
....
....
....
....
....
....
....
....
....
....
....
....
....
....

Exercise Chapter 7

Write a list of your qualities

....
....
....
....
....
....
....
....
....
....
....
....
....
....
....
....
....
....
....
....
....
....
....
....
....
....
....
....

Exercise Chapter 8

Take a few long deep breaths, then channel your inner voice onto paper. Write about anything. Write about whatever it is that crosses your mind. This is your Higher Self sending you a message. Write about good or bad.

....
....
....
....
....
....
....
....
....
....
....
....
....
....
....
....
....
....
....
....
....
....
....
....

Exercise Chapter 10

Write three things you are grateful for.

1.

2.

3.

Exercise Chapter 10

Write the pros and cons of one decision you need to make today.

DECISION	
PROS	CONS

Exercise Chapter 10

Write your favorite affirmations and repeat them throughout the day.

....
....
....
....
....
....
....
....
....
....
....
....
....
....
....
....
....
....
....
....
....
....
....
....
....
....
....
....
....

Resources

- Writing from the source - Techniques for Re-scripting your Life - Allison Price
- Walking on sunshine - 52 Small Steps to Happiness - Rachel Kelly
- Writing down the bones - Freeing the Writer Within - Natalie Goldberg
- How of Happiness - Sonja Lyubomirsky
- If You're So Smart, Why Aren't You Happy? - Raj Raghunathan
- The Dynamic Way of Meditation - Dhiravamsa
- Ann Hood TEDxProvince 2015- "Why Write?": https://www.youtube.com/watch?v=nvdsu2KMhno
- Thordis Elva and Tom Stranger TED Women 2016 - "Our story of rape and reconciliation": https://www.ted.com/talks/thordis_elva_tom_stranger_our_story_of_rape_and_reconciliation
- The Secret - Rhonda Byrne and Think and Grow Rich - Napoleon Hill on The Law of Attraction

Acknowledgements

Special thanks to my mentors Professor Raj Raghunathan, Rachel Kelly and Professor James W. Pennebaker for agreeing to offer me interviews as part of the research for this book.

A massive thank you to all my supportive friends. Also my parents, who I've dedicated this book to, because they have always been proud of me, even though they don't quite understand what it is that I'm doing.